From the Cotton Fields
to a College Professor

From the Cotton Fields to a College Professor

My Life's Experience

Dr. Joe H. Alcorta

Library of Congress Control Number:		2011903569
ISBN:	Hardcover	978-1-4568-8172-6
	Softcover	978-1-4568-8171-9
	Ebook	978-1-4568-8173-3

To order additional copies of this book, contact:
Xlibris Corporation
1-888-795-4274
www.Xlibris.com
Orders@Xlibris.com
90841

Contents

A Note of Appreciation

My special thanks go to the following people:

My wife, Liandra, who always supports and encourages me in my everyday activities.

She is my biggest fan. She reads and proofreads everything I write.

To my four children, Cecilia Yvette Castillo, Joe, Jr., Samuel Adriel, and Daniel Andres who support and encourage me in my many adventures. My daughter and three sons are an inspiration to me. All four contributed to the writing of this book.

To my parents, Mr. and Mrs. Richard Alcorta, Sr., who worked hard and sacrificed so that I and my brothers and sisters could have a good life. Even though they did not have an education, they insisted that we stay in school to better ourselves. They modeled the Christian faith to me.

To Rev. Glen E. Godsey and his wife, Oralia, for providing great Christian leadership and encouragement in my young Christian life. Bro. Godsey served as pastor at my church, Mision Bautista La Trinidad, in Olton, Texas.

To Mr. Glenn Dromgoole, author and former editor of *The Abilene Reporter-News,* Abilene, Texas, who gave me my first opportunity to write essays for the editorial page in *The Reporter-News.*

To my other church pastors and their families for their encouragement: Rev. and Mrs. Dale Suel, Rev. and Mrs. T.C. Melton, Rev. and Mrs. Bill Ybarra, Rev. and Mrs. Victor Ortiz, Rev. and Mrs. Lester Vinson, and Rev. and Mrs. David McQueen.

To my elementary, high school, and college teachers who took an interest in me and told me many times: "You can do it!"

To Earl Garrett, J.T. Box, Travis Seekins, Troy Cartwright, Brenda Harris, and Janlyn Thaxton, all fellow workers here at Hardin-Simmons University who helped me in a great way in producing this book.

A big special thanks to Kassia Jackson, a former student of mine and now a colleague, for proofreading all the manuscript, for her valuable suggestions, and for writing the introduction to this book.

Introduction

One could write a book on Dr. Alcorta's accomplishments alone. Dr. Alcorta has written several books, including *Words of Wisdom from a Cool College Professor*, and a history of the Dallas Cowboys in Spanish. He has participated in many marathons, running even at the age of seventy! He has raised a beautiful and supportive family as well as acquired a masters and doctorate degree. However, these honors are not what students think about when they enter Dr. Alcorta's classroom. Being in Dr. Alcorta's class is comparable to coming home and having a cup of coffee with your dad. In fact, many students, including myself, affectionately refer to Dr. Alcorta as "Pappa Joe" because he wants all his students to know that he loves them.

Readers will find many letters in this autobiography confirming the manner in which Dr. Alcorta teaches his students. He truly cares about the students' lives not just the classroom material. Many times he takes time aside to pray with students or to mentor them individually. Students leave his classroom not only having learned a little Spanish, but having gained a confidant and spiritual counselor, which is why students feel compelled to keep in touch with Dr. Alcorta even after leaving the forty acres of Hardin Simmons University.

Students spend hours in Dr. Alcorta's office, discussing their lives, triumphs, and struggles, but Dr. Alcorta's latest book reveals the stories of his own journey from cotton picker to college professor. He discusses his challenges, such as experiencing racism in the school systems or the loss of his beloved sister, Rachel. He talks about his personal victories, such as becoming the first Hispanic member of the Abilene city council or graduating from Texas Tech with a PhD. He discusses his love for his students and for his family often linking the two together. He also shares personal information, such as the manuscripts of his family newsletter or family recipes. The book is a legacy for his family and for his students, but it is also a testament to what people can accomplish if they have a little faith. It is a chance for students and readers alike to enjoy a glimpse into this inspiring man's life . . . . and what a life it has been!

—Kassia Jackson

God Wants Us to Succeed

God has a great sense of humor. A popular Christian song says, "Where a man sees a shepherd boy, God sees a King." Certainly I am not a king but with God's help and guidance I have come a long way from the hot cotton fields of Olton, Texas where I pulled a 12-foot cotton sack all day long.

God has great plans for all of us! Did you read that? I will tell you again: God has great plans for all of us. He wants us to prosper, have success, and enjoy life to the fullest. That does not mean that we will not have any problems or challenges. Problems and challenges happen every day to everybody! The only big catch is that God wants us to succeed His way! And that's where most people go wrong.

People go after education, wealth, power, and name to succeed. But many put the cart before the horse. God wants to be first! That is what Jesus says in the Sermon on the Mount: "Seek ye first the kingdom of God and His righteousness and all these things shall be added unto you" (Matthew 6:33).

The Apostle John says: "Love not the world, neither the things that are in the world. If any man loves the world, the love of the Father is not in him. For all that is in the world, the lust of the flesh, and the lust of the eyes, and the pride of life, is not of the Father, but is of the world"—(I John 2:15, 16).

Many times in the Bible God blessed Joseph because he was faithful and loyal to God in all circumstances. Joseph, hated by his brothers, was sold as a slave. As a slave and servant, Joseph, was falsely accused by a woman and was put in jail. Regardless of all that happened to Joseph he remained faithful to God. At the end his life, he was second in command under the powerful King Herod.

God's instructions to Joshua as he is preparing to lead the liberated Israelites from Egyptian reads as follows:

"This book of the law shall not depart from your mouth, but you shall meditate on it day and night, so that you may be careful to do according to all that is written in it; for then you will make your way prosperous, and then you will have success."

—Joshua 1:8.

I try very hard to follow and obey the above Scriptures in my own life. A few years ago I told my wife: "I am through buying unnecessary things. I do not want a new car, boat, gun, etc." Every day I work hard at memorizing Scripture and then work harder at obeying it. God rewards obedience.

In this book, with God's help, I hope to share my story. Everyone has a story to tell. I would want to tell my story so that it will help you and others when things get rough and tough. We live in a tough world, and we all will face problems and challenges. Regardless of how close you are to God, you will have problems.

The big difference is how you and others respond and react to the different problems. Every problem has a solution and something to be learned from it. So, when a problem or a challenge comes up, ask God, "Okay, God, what am I supposed to learn from this situation?" Other questions to ask might be: "Okay, what happened?" "Why did it happen?" "Could it have been avoided?"

My Parents Background

My Mother's (Maria de Jesus Quiroz Alcorta) grandparents were from Allende, Mexico. The grandmother's name was Ildefonsa Minor Quiroz; she was a seamstress. The grandfather was a very rough, jealous, and strict man. When the oldest daughter of the family married, he (the grandfather) prohibited the family to ever see that sister again. So, the family never knew anything about the oldest daughter.

Ildefonsa Minor Quiroz (my Mother's grandmother) died giving birth to a baby girl. At that time, my Mother's mother, Maria de los Angeles Quiroz was 15 years old. The grandfather became even stricter after the death of his wife with the family, and he did not permit the girls to go to school. Grandmother wanted to learn to read and write, and she began to ask her younger brother who was permitted to go to school about his lessons in school. She and her brother would read in hiding. She learned to read but not to write. She always talked about a special brother that she respected and admired a great deal, and would always refer to him as "Mi hermano." (My brother).

Sometimes my Mother's grandfather would beat his daughter (Maria de los Angeles Quiroz) for any kind of reason. Maria de los Angeles Quiroz could no longer take this kind of life (the beating and rough treatment) and she ran away from home, and began to serve a rich family as a maid with the idea that the family would take her with them to the United States.

My grandmother, Maria de los Angeles Quiroz and the rich family arrived in Del Rio, Texas in 1913. In Del Rio, Maria de los Angeles began to work, and the family she was living with decided to return to Mexico. My grandmother did not want to return to Mexico, and she stayed with another family that offered her work.

In Del Rio, my grandmother began to see this businessman, Andres Rodriguez, who had a meat market. He was related to the rich family that she had come with to the states. The businessman man was tall, well built, dark complexted, and very handsome. In secret Maria de los Angeles Quiroz began to see this man, and soon my Mother, Maria, was born (in the year 1915) out of that relationship.

Maria Alcorta (my Mother) said about her father: "Oh, how I wish I would have known more about my Father, but all I know is that he abandoned me the day I was born. But I have forgiven him and I love him, but still, one of my greatest desires was to have known my father."

After my grandmother and Mother were abandoned, grandmother went to live with a woman that took care of Mother as if she was her granddaughter, while Mother worked. Two years later, in 1917, grandmother married Porfirio Soliz who adopted Mother as his daughter. From this marriage Antonio, Maria Ester, Porfirio, Juanita, and Jose were born. Grandmother left this man because of a very justified reason. Later, grandmother married Longino Villa, and from this marriage Isabel, Alejandro, Rosa, Longino, and Rafael were born.

My Mother, Maria Alcorta, said: "I was born in Del Rio, Texas, with very few opportunities. During my childhood we lived in ranches where there were cattle and other animals and for that reason I learned to love animals. I feel sorry when someone mistreats any kind of animal. I also like trees, rocks, hills, mountains, and rivers. In the countryside I spent my childhood playing under a tree, with rocks, making believe that I had a ranch with many herds of cattle and horses, and hens, and doves."

This upbringing of my Mother helped in her daily living. She learned to improvise and to do without some things. She could fix us a meal with very few groceries.

Dad, Ricardo Alcorta, was born in Rome, Texas. His parents were Ricardo and Irene Alcorta. His brothers and sisters were: Luciano, Victoria and Isabel.

Grandmother Alcorta then married Pedro Gauna from where she had the following children: Francisca, Candido, Irenio and Plutarco. Along the way, the families fought and argued about something, and family members split on the spelling of their last name; some said "Gauna," and the others said, "Gaona." In Sweetwater, I knew both families as Gauna and Gaona.

Ricardo was a hard working person and grew up doing all kinds of manual work around the farm. He remembers driving a pair of mules in the fields. Later in life, Ricardo, drove a modern tractor in the cotton fields of Roscoe Thomas in Olton, Texas. There was no time for school so he never attended school. Not one day! He could not read or write. Later in life he taught himself how to read in Spanish by reading the Bible.

From Rome, Grandpa Alcorta went to Bridge Port to work in the mines. Grandma Alcorta would sell tamales and tacos for extra income. From there they moved to Ft. Worth and then to Dallas.

Dad Falls in Love with Mom

Dad (Ricardo Alcorta) and Mom (Maria de Jesus Quiroz) met for the first time during a stormy night at Caps near Abilene, Texas. Mother's parents, Longino Villa and his wife Maria were travelling in a covered Model-T truck going to Novice, Texas, in 1930. It was very cold and raining. The Villas stopped at the Alcortas ranch, outside of Abilene in Caps for help and lodging.

First, Dad's brother, Irenio, went out and he told the traveling family that there was no room in the house. Then Dad (Ricardo) came out and he noticed a baby in the back of the covered Model T. The newborn was Rosa Villa, sister of Maria (my Mother). Dad went back into the house and told his Mother that there was a baby in the Model T. His Mother, said, "Okay, ask them to come in." That night Dad looked into Mother's eyes and it was love at first sight. They stayed with the Alcorta family for 15 days and they took advantage to work by pulling cotton.

Dad and mother married young on November 17, 1931 near Abilene, Texas. Dad was 19, and Mother was 16. In fact, they eloped. They were married in a farm house by a Baptist minister. Dad went and picked up Mother on a bicycle from her house one night. Dad and mother lived with his Mother (Irene Ocon) and family. Mother said her two sisters'-in-law, Isabel and Victoria (sisters of my Dad) were real mean to her.

The first child born to Ricardo and Maria was Margarita who was born in Spur, Texas, in Dickens County on September 5, 1932. Maria hand-made all of Margarita's clothes. The next child was Maria who was born on November 23, 1936, but she only lived two hours. Ricardo was born premature in 1936 (dead when born); Juanito, lived 8 days, born on August 14, 1938; and Juan Enrique, born 1941, lived 2 years and 9 months. Juan Enrique died in Mexico.

Julia, the third child, was born on April 2, 1935. The first boy born to the family was Ricardo on May 19, 1937.

I was born in a humble house in Novice, Texas, (60 miles from Abilene) on October 22, 1939. Novice was a real small town composed of a grocery store, a few business firms and the doctor's office. Dr. Kidd of Novice was the M.D. who came to our house and delivered me. I was born at 6:00 o'clock in the morning, and I weigh between 6 and 7 pounds. At the time of my birth, Dad was working in the fields doing manual labor.

My stay in Novice was not long as we moved to Mexico the same year, two months later. Dad says we arrived in Mexico on January 1, 1940.

Living in Mexico

When I was two months old, our family packed up and moved to Zuazua, Nuevo Leon, Mexico. My grandmother, Maria Quiroz Villa, was afraid that the military (it was during WW I) might draft her son Porfirio (Pilo) and she talked her family into moving to Mexico. At this time, Longino and Maria invited Ricardo Alcorta (my Dad) and family to go with them. Ricardo accepted and later wanted to back out but it was too late. He had already given his word.

Mother used to tell me that her friends in Mexico, would often tell her about me, "Send him to school and educate him, he is going to be a good one."

So for about 7 or 8 years we lived in Zuazua and Monterrey, Nuevo Leon, Mexico. Dad worked in Monterrey in a ranch with Mr. Vicente Quiroga in a dairy where we had to milk about 50 cows every day early in the morning. Dad also learned to work with oxen and to wear huaraches. Later he worked on public roads driving a truck in road construction.

In Zuazua we lived in a very small adobe house my Dad made with his own hands. There was no door, so at night Mother would sleep across the door for protection. We had no electricity or running water. There was a river about a mile away where we obtained water. At the river, Richard, my oldest brother would catch turtles so we could eat them.

In Zuazua during the summer in the afternoons we used to go to the river to bath and swim; and then we would eat aguacates (avocados) and tortillas for supper. Sometimes Mother would make a salad of tomatoes and onions. In those days, we liked everything. After supper we would sing "coritos" that we had learned from a Pentecostal church whose pastor was Eusebio Alcala. They called the preacher "Hermano Dulcero" ("Brother Candy Man") because he made candy; we helped him to wrap and sell the candy so he would share it with us.

Mother was a very good seamstress, and in Mexico, necessity required that she continue sewing. She made shirts, pants, and dresses—all the clothes we needed.

In August, 1946, my Mother, Julia, Luisa, and Martha came to McAllen, Texas, from Mexico to work and help support the family. Mother had promised to buy us a tricycle and that is why we thought it was worth while waiting for. But she couldn't very well afford to buy them and much less carry them with her back to Mexico. Mother worked in the fields pulling cotton. Also with them were Mother's brother and sister, Jose and Juanita Solis. From McAllen they went to Big Spring to follow the cotton crops. They lived in a chicken coop behind the house of the owner. Mother became ill; she seemed to have had a stroke.

Mr. and Mrs. Crespin Chapa (my uncle and aunt) somehow found out that Mother and daughters were working in Big Spring. Crespin and Victoria went for Mother and took her to Dallas where they found her a job cleaning shrimp. There in Dallas they began making plans to bring the family from Mexico to the United States.

Back in Mexico, Margarita (Mague) our oldest sister took care of my brother Richard and me. She did the cooking, washing, and cleaning. In Mexico, I remember Mague going to the store on Saturday mornings to buy "galletas de vainilla" (vanilla wafers) for breakfast. That was a treat!

Dad would wake up very early every day to go to work. One early morning no one was awake and I by the grace of God I awoke. I saw fire in the kitchen. Our small house was burning. I made noise to get everyone's attention and immediately Dad got up and put out the fire.

In school I was always afraid and shy. Since my sister Mague attended the same elementary school (Mariano Escobedo) during recess, I hung around with her. I would not let her out of my sight! I completed first grade in Suazua and was in second grade in Monterrey when we returned to Dallas, Texas, in 1946. In the two years in school I learned to read and write in Spanish. That turned out to be very helpful and beneficial in my future career as a teacher of Spanish.

I don't remember it but Mom would tell us that it was in Mexico that our little brother, Enrique died at the age of 3, because we did not have the money for his medicine. Mom had walked all the way to the doctor's office, and then she had to walk all the way back home. My brother died in my Mom's arms before she got home.

Two of my sisters, Luisa and Martha were born in Mexico. Luisa was born on August 25, 1943; and Martha was born on August 21, 1945.

Crespin and Victoria Chapa

Uncle Crespin Chapa and his wife, Victoria, went to Mexico to bring our family back to the states. I believe we had tried returning earlier in 1943, but we did not have the necessary papers. I am very grateful that God used the Chapas to bring our family back to the states. When we came back to the states, we only had the clothes on our back and that was all. In 1943 we had sold everything and then we had nothing when we could not come across. So this time, Dad thought it best to leave everything just in case!

It was my uncle Crespin who encouraged me in a great way. While in the fields pulling cotton, he would tell me, "You need to go to school so you can wear nice slacks, a white shirt and have a good job." When we were in Dallas, I spent a lot of time with them. I was their "favorite nephew."

I remember a funny story I would like to share. My uncle and aunt often would fight and have discussions. One day during an argument, my aunt grabbed a can full of gasoline with matches in hand and she was chasing my uncle in the house. My uncle kept repeating: "No Negas, que tienes! Estas loca?" (Don't Honey, what is wrong with you! Are you crazy?)

It was my uncle Crespin who taught me how to drive in his 1936 Ford. I learned to drive in the cotton fields where it was safe. It was my aunt Chapa who bought me my wedding suit in Dallas, Texas. In fact, my aunt also wanted to buy Liandra's wedding ring but Liandra didn't think it was a good idea.

To say that the Chapas did a lot for our family is an understatement. My sisters Mague and Martha lived with them in Dallas while they worked in the big city.

The Chapas could not have children of their own so later in life they adopted two girls: Esperanza and Yolanda. Both girls had children, and when the Chapas died they left me as the executor of their will. They left around $30,000 in savings so I could distribute to the girls and the grandchildren when they became of legal age. They also left their home to Yolanda. Crespin and Victoria died in 1999.

In Dallas we lived in a tent in the property of my aunt Francisca Rios where Grandmother (Dad's Mother) was living. We attended a Catholic school where I was in the first grade. None of us knew English which was a real challenge at school. Josie and Frank Rios, our cousins, were our interpreters in school. One day after school, the nuns took us to downtown Dallas to buy us clothes. Boy that was a big blessing. I still remember a blue and red corduroy jacket they bought me. I kept the two jackets for a long time. At Christmas time again they bought us a lot of things.

Living in Sweetwater, Texas

In 1947, after grandmother passed away in Dallas, we moved to Sweetwater with my uncle Candido Gauna, (half-brother of my Dad) his wife Florinda and all of their family. My uncle Gauna came for us from Sweetwater to Dallas in a red Dodge. There were like 12 in their family. The Gauna family consisted of Eduardo, Isabel (Chavela), Blas, Elizabet, Manuel, Pablo, Marta, Maria, Florinda, Francisco (Frank), Florencio, and Eugenio. I can remember like if it was today, the first night we slept on the floor, and under the beds I saw several bottles of milk with nipples on them! Some of our cousins were grown but they were still on the bottle!

My uncle Candido and aunt Florinda had their kitchen outside separate from the main house. There my aunt and her daughters cooked the meals. I can still remember that large big stack of flour tortillas that were made every day! They got up at 4:00 a.m. every day to cook breakfast. In the afternoon after coming back from work, my dad, uncle and cousins would go hunting for rabbits. It seemed like we had rabbit to eat every day!! My uncle Gauna and his older sons (Eduardo, Blas, Manuel, and Pablo) took care of the farm/ranch. They planted cotton, wheat, and hay. They worked real hard. I believe they worked on a percentage basis with their boss and owner of the farm.

I not only got to develop my relationship with my family in Sweetwater, but my relationship with the Lord as well. It was in a ranch revival in 1948 in Sweetwater where I accepted Jesus Christ as my Savior. The pastor of the small mission was the Rev. Victor Ortiz. Brother Ortiz was a student at Hardin-Simmons University where he had started at the age of 50! He graduated from Hardin-Simmons University in 1952. Bro. Ortiz baptized me at First Baptist Church, Sweetwater because our small church did not have a baptistery.

In school in Sweetwater, our second pastor, Rev. Lester Vinson came up with the idea that he would give me a nickel for every 100 I would make in school. Well, I made a lot of them, and so the H-SU student minister, Bro. Vinson kindly backed away! But I appreciate Bro. Vinson very much for encouraging me in school.

He was the first Anglo who took me to a white barbershop in Sweetwater. At that time barbers did not cut the hair of "Mexicans." Well, Bro. Vinson took me with the idea that he was ready to fight if they did not cut my hair. Needless to say, they did not say anything, because I was with an Anglo minister! He and his wife Peggy had much influence on our family. I remember spending many nights in their home in Abilene.

My uncle Candido was not for church, and his family wanted to have a service in their ranch so he could hear the Gospel. When the preacher arrived, my uncle left the house through the back door. Later my uncle Candido died in a car accident travelling to or from San Angelo. I never knew if he was saved or not. My uncle Candido was very strict with his family, especially the girls. He would not let them date or go anywhere unless it was with their Mother. My uncle Candido on the weekend would drive to San Angelo to buy beer. At that time no alcohol was sold in Nolan County.

In Sweetwater, Dad got a job in Roby as a farm hand. It was here in Roby that I started again in the first grade. A school bus came at our ranch and took us to school. That first day, after school I was completely confused. I did not know or did not remember my bus number or if there was any number. Well after school, I got on the wrong bus. I could not speak English so I could not communicate. After the bus driver left everyone home, he drove back to school and that is where Dad found me. My brother and sister had arrived home already and told Dad that I was not on the bus.

In Roby, Mr. Brascum, my Dad's boss, helped Margarita, Julia, Richard, and Joe to obtain their birth certificates and made them U.S. citizens. Margarita, especially, needed her birth certificate since she needed to attend the Mexican Baptist Valley Academy in Harlingen, Texas. It is not known why the birth certificates of Luisa and Martha were not taken into consideration to become U.S. citizens. Both girls were born in Mexico. Luisa was born in Suazua, and Martha was born in Monterrey.

Our first car was a nice 1937 Chevrolet. We all were real proud of it and it lasted us for several years. Our next car was a 1940 Chevrolet that lasted for another six years. It was on this 1940 model that I paid a lot of money. Daddy would take what I made during the week in the fields and pay on the car—he said it was mine.

Emiliano Carranza Elementary

From Roby we moved to Sweetwater where Dad got a job in a supermarket. We again started school. The school, Emiliano Carranza, was a school for "the Mexican" children. At that time the Mexicans could not attend school with the Anglos. Here I believe they placed me in the second grade and that same year promoted me to third or fourth. The school was horrible. It was a building with four large rooms. I believe third and fourth were together; as were fifth and sixth. There was no discipline whatsoever.

I remember the first or second grade teacher's name was Ms. Monk. All I can remember about her was hearing her say over and over "Hush! Hush" as she placed her index finger in her mouth. I think Mr. Sturch was my fifth grade teacher. We had no playground whatsoever. When it rained there was mud in the playground. My cousins, the Gaunas, also attended this school. A big yellow school bus would bring them from the ranch.

Most days after school the kids would meet at the hill and fight. I remember one time it was my cousin Aurora Gaona and some girl really got into a fight. It was awful. The next day at school they were really bruised and scratched.

It was so bad that we told our Dad that there was no discipline in school. Dad went and told the Sweetwater school administration, and either the principal or the superintendent came to our school, Emiliano Carranza, to improve on the discipline. It only lasted that day that the superintendent came.

During the summer that we were out of school, we would work chopping cotton or working in yards or just doing odd jobs. We usually pulled cotton up to December and then start school and at times it was real difficult to catch up in school. It wasn't until the seventh grade that I started school in September, and that was in Olton. We would usually pull cotton in Sweetwater and then go elsewhere to continue working. During the years we traveled to Liberty Hill, Georgetown, Waco, Temple, Tyler, Cameron, Floydada, and Olton. We had many, many experiences living in old houses, barns, and old shacks. There were a lot of things that went on in all these different places that we lived. Sometimes we were stung by scorpions when we slept on the floor.

My life was not all work and no play. Most every night we would play bingo, cards, dominoes, or "la loteria." Usually the rounds were one cent, and then the last games were of a nickel or a dime. Then of course, when it rained that was about all we did. The real big gambling went on Friday,

Saturday, and Sunday nights. On the weekends most of the men would be drinking.

In Sweetwater, we worshiped at the Spanish Baptist Mission where Rev. Lester Vinson and Rev. Victor Ortiz were pastors. The mission was sponsored by First Baptist Church in Sweetwater. Both, Bro. Vinson and Bro. Ortiz were HSU students. It was Bro. Ortiz who took us to our first church camp. Dad had a small trailer and the preacher used it to take us to a church family camp in Menard, Texas. Brother Silva was the camp minister. This was and is a Mexican camp owned by Hispanics. It was a real camp as we did not have cabins or buildings. We camped out in tents! The worship service was in an open building called "el tabernaculo" (the tabernacle). There was no air condition or running water. We took cold showers from a hanging hose in a make-shift small building.

When I came to HSU in 1960 I went to this same camp in Menard and there I met Daniel Rivera. Daniel, myself and others slept on top of the kitchen which was partly covered. I also remember getting up early and singing "Las mañanitas to the girls." Our swimming pool for the camp was the river! I remember there was a long rope from a tree where people would use to jump into the river. Daniel currently (2010) is a seminary professor at the Baptist Theological Seminary at Ft. Worth, Texas. Daniel and I have kept in touch.

Living in Olton, Texas

I completed the fifth grade at Emiliano Carranza and then we moved to Olton, Texas, which is about fifty miles north of Lubbock. As was customary during the summers, we were working in the fields hoeing. Mr. Victoriano Gutierrez asked Dad if we could go with him to Olton, Texas, to pull cotton. Dad was working in a grocery store in Sweetwater and he could not go. So, Julia, Richard, and I went with the Gutierrez to Olton, in 1951. In Olton we lived in barracks on the outskirts of town. The barracks was one building in a straight line with eight rooms. A couple of months later, Dad and Mom and the rest of the family came to Olton.

Daddy and Mother had stayed in Sweetwater along with the small children. Julia, Richard and myself came to Olton with Victor Gutierrez (el troquero-truck driver), with us also came my aunts, Ester Sandoval, Juanita Soliz, and Rosa Villa. We lived in a brand new barracks built and owned by Burl Willis, the man we were to work for. Here in this barracks everything went—dancing, cursing, gambling, drinking, boot legging—you name it—it was here in this barracks. There were 8 rooms in all. In fact one day several policemen came to the barracks with a search warrant and wanted to know if we were selling beer. Mother said: "Not us!" but she also told the policemen who was selling beer at the barracks! They found lots of it!

That first winter (1951-52) in Olton was very hard. It snowed, froze and there was lot of ice. We did not know anyone. Times were very hard. Richard (Rico), my oldest brother, did not like school so he lied about his age and got a job with Mr. Roscoe Thomas driving a tractor and doing different types of work on the farm. Through Rico, Roscoe asked Dad to go and work for him. So, we moved to his farm. He furnished us with a small house plus utilities where we lived. Dad's salary was $150.00 a month plus 10 acres of land which he could farm.

All of our family helped Dad by working in the cotton fields. We mainly pulled cotton or hoed cotton. I was very good at pulling cotton. If the cotton crop was good, I could pull 1000 pounds in a day. We normally would get paid from $1.50 to $2.00 per hundred pounds. We also would go in a truck to Hereford, Texas, to plant onions, pick tomatoes and potatoes. Because of work we would start school in November, and for that reason we would always be behind in our school studies.

At that time, Mother was pregnant with our baby sister Rachel. Dad had asked Roscoe if he could borrow $150 to prepare for hospital expenses. Roscoe said yes. Rachel was born in the Olton hospital on March 29, 1952.

It was in Olton that we met Rev. Glen Godsey and his wife Oralia. Bro. Glen was the pastor of the small Mexican Baptist Mission. The mission was an old abandon Army headquarters that had been purchased by members of the local First Baptist Church. The building was fenced with weeds higher than the building itself. This church starting from scraps began with four members, Bro. Godsey, his wife, and two other unknown persons. It grew to have over 200 members by the time Bro. Godsey left in 1960. Bro. Glen and his wife loved the Lord and they did so much for the people of Olton. Bro. Glen was attending Wayland Baptist College while he was pastor in Olton.

Bro. Glen taught me so much about the Bible and Christian living. We had Sunday school, Brotherhood, Women Missionary Union, Girls Auxiliaries, Sunbeams, and youth activities. Every January we would participate in the annual Baptist Convention Bible study. We attended Associational meetings on Saturday or Sunday afternoon. The young people would also have their meetings. At times I was their president or their leader. Mrs. Roscoe Thomas was one of our Sunday school teachers. It was through her that Rico got a job with her husband Roscoe; and she found me a job at The Olton Enterprise.

Bro. Glen from the pulpit preached against going to the movies. He said they were worldly and evil and for that reason I did not attend the movies while he was my pastor. I respected him so much.

In 1955 Mother went to Monterrey, Mexico to visit her Mother and other relatives. When she returned it was discovered that Rachel had polio. At that time no one knew much about polio. Rachel was placed in a Plainview hospital and no family member was permitted to stay with her, not even Mother. It was Rev. Glen Godsey that started praying and asking everyone around the community to pray for Rachel's healing. And that is what happened! Rachel was healed!

(It was ironic that 50 years later I would be participating in a program with our local Abilene Rotary Club and Rotary International to eradicate polio around the world. Rotary International has raised over $500,000,000, and polio is nearly eradicated. Praise the Lord! I remember those sad days in our home when our little sister was in a Plainview hospital)

Roscoe Thomas and his wife Bert were great people. They helped us so much. At the beginning of school, we normally would stay and work in the fields the months of August, September and October. Roscoe told my Dad: "Richard, those children need to be in school. School is very important." So, thanks to Roscoe and Bert, we started school in September.

At times when we were sick, Mrs. Thomas would come over to our house with a syringe and penicillin and gave us injections. We children did not like it at all!!! But, our parents appreciated that very much. Mrs. Thomas also was our Sunday school teacher at La Mision Bautista la Trinidad in Olton.

I started school in Olton in the 6th grade. It was very hard at first because we had come from a poor school situation (back in Sweetwater, Emilio Carranza), and we would always start school late in November. Rico really got discouraged and quit; he told Dad that he would rather work than go to school.

When I started school in Olton most of my grades were in the seventies, and a few eighties. About at the end of the year my grades started going higher. My seventh and eighth grades were average. My highest grades were in arithmetic and spelling. I guess the most fun of my school life was in the seventh and eighth grade. Lennon Young, a close friend of mine, and I had a ball in school with Mrs. Lila Wall, our history teacher and homeroom teacher. She liked us a lot! Mrs. Wall would name someone to take names of students who were acting up in class during the day and when Lennon or I got elected, he or I could do just whatever we wanted. We were put in the hall several times, but we always knew what the limit was; we always avoided the principal's office!

Mrs. Collar was my reading and spelling teacher. I would make hundreds most of the time in spelling, but I would write so small that she had to take my papers right close to her nose to see what was written. One day she got tired of telling me about my small writing and she just took my paper and gave me a zero.

My sophomore year was a little different. I took Algebra II, English II, biology, and American History. During that year I had two hundreds in my report card; one in American History, and the other in Algebra II. I enjoyed English during my sophomore year also. I think my English teacher, Mrs. Ruth Ford, was the best teacher I had. By this I mean from what I learned from her. I think she was very strict with us. She was known to be the hardest teacher in OHS; I loved her, though. The grammar part—I give credit to Mrs. John Campbell, she had been my English teacher in the seventh and eighth grade, and to me most of the grammar was the same. Mrs. John Campbell was the first or second best teacher as far as teaching is concerned. That year as usual, I passed all my subjects, but again biology this time was getting me down, boy those bugs really got me down; I think I passed the last semester with a 73.

My junior year I had just about all my required subjects taken during my first two years; so this year I took English III, Typing I, Plane Geometry, and Chemistry. I don't know why I took chemistry; I honestly think I didn't have a choice. Anyway, I think I passed it with a 70. Typing I, Plane geometry, and English came along with flying colors, but chemistry was the headache.

A great thrill for me in high school was when Mrs. Ford, the sponsor of the National Honor Society, informed me that I had been chosen as a candidate for membership in the National Honor Society, or that is to say the Principal's Honor Roll. I was shocked and thrilled. A student was selected by the faculty and approved by the superintendent and the principal. A student had to have at least an 85 average, and must demonstrate good leadership abilities plus having good moral standards. Not only was I approved but I was elected its president the last semester of my high school year.

My senior year was the greatest, not only was I a member of the National Honor Society, but its president also; and then too was elected favorite of my class. My senior year I took Civics, Texas History, English IV, Typing II, and Physics. Boy did Physics give me pains! It even took me to the principal's office for the first time in my life! I had been to the principal's office before but not something like this. It was during the last semester, and I think we had about a month and a half of school. My attention was called to me that I was failing physics. I knew I was; but we were being encouraged by our dear principal, Mr. J.W. Williams, that I couldn't graduate without it. My highest grade during my senior year was in English.

As president of the NHS I presided over the ceremony before the whole student body in honoring those students during the year that had made the A and B roll. I was rather nervous, but excited.

Another honor that I received in high school was been class favorite along with Shirley Webb—one of my best girl friends in school. She was real sweet and smart. She finished ranking 3rd in our class but I think she should have been valedictorian since she took four years of science and four years of math.

By the 8th grade I began to catch up and started competing with my classmates. I really did well in math. I loved it. It was in the 8th or 9th grade that I started to compete in the Interscholastic Number Sense.

In Number Sense a student had 100 math with some algebra problems to solve. The student had only 10 minutes to complete the test, and the only thing a student could write was the answer. In other words, a student had to solve the problems in his head and then write the answer down. Every tenth problem, a student could miss the answer by 10% and be given credit. There were different types of tests. Most of the harder ones, no one could finish.

In Olton High School, most mornings two or three of us would go early to the class of Mr. Fischer where he helped us with the math problems. We all worked together and learned how to do short cuts in solving the problems. We learned the multiplication tables from one to twenty-five. We could square any number and get the correct answer in our head. We knew easily how to multiply any number by twenty-five, fifty, or seventy-five. At one time we learned how to multiply three digits by three digits. We knew the percentages and fractions backwards and forwards. We knew many formulas. I still remember that a car travelling at sixty miles an hour will cover eighty-eight feet per second!

I won District in Number Sense two or three years in a row. From District we would go to Regional. One year, my partner, Emery Hughes went all the way to the state meet in Austin. Wow! That was exciting! He did not win, but we all enjoyed the competition and the travel to Austin. As a reward, one year after school in June Mr. Fischer took four of us boys in his covered pickup on a fishing trip to the coast at Port Aransas. We went deep sea fishing! It was a great trip.

I really enjoyed my high school days in Olton. I had great teachers. I especially liked Mr. Ford, the math teacher. From Mr. Ford I took Algebra I, Algebra II, Geometry and Physics. He was a great teacher. There were two or three of who were outstanding in the class, and Mr. Ford often would give us challenging problems to solve. I really loved math. I did not have Mr. Fischer for a class, but I also liked him a lot and learned much from him when he coached us in Number Sense.

I saw Mr. Ford several times after I graduated. He attended our classes' reunions in Olton. One year I saw him at Howard Payne in Brownwood. I was an honoree (outstanding Hispanic Howard Payne alumni) and was riding in the parade. From the crowd, Mr. Ford addresses me and says, "Hi Joe!" I was so surprised and excited that I made the float stop, got out and went and shook the hand of Mr. Ford. Boy that was something!

In 2007, I was surprised and honored to have received a party invitation and a phone call to celebrate the 95th birthday of Mr. Ford in Littlefield, Texas. My wife and I attended and we had a great time. Mr. Ford and I took a great picture! In fact, it was published in *The Abilene Reporter-News*. Three years later I returned to attend his funeral. He lived to be 99!

Mr. Howton was my typing teaching teacher. I took two years of typing. I was good at it! I believe I was able to type 40 and then 60 words per minute. The typewriter that I used in my classroom I was able to buy it because the school was buying electric typewriters. Then when I was working at the Olton Enterprise, my boss, Troy Martin, rented the typewriter from me at $5.00 per month. Wow! I still have that manual Royal typewriter!!!

I was always involved in our church in Olton. I was also working at *The Olton Enterprise*. Sometimes, I would work as much as 40 hours. It was rough! And more than once did I think of quitting school but there was my Mother all the time to insist that I keep on (actually, she said I could quit if I wanted to, because she knew what I was going through). Troy Martin (my boss) always told me to leave work if necessary to keep up with my lessons or to attend church. I did leave work to do the latter but not the first. My Sunday evening would be spent by either working on my lessons or catching up on my sleep. I missed my senior trip and one or two class parties because I felt I could not afford it. I would have to pay the expenses to go and then I would lose that much more from not working. I figured my Senior trip would cost me more than double it if I did go.

Working at The Olton Enterprise

In Olton, during my freshman year, I began to work part-time at our weekly newspaper, *The Olton Enterprise*. It was Mrs. Roscoe Thomas who got me the job. My boss, Troy Martin, saw something in me, and he said he wanted to hire me full time. It was here in the newspaper that I learned to operate a linotype, a machine used to set type for printing purposes.

My first few days at *The Olton Enterprise* were to clean up the place! It was dirty! There was paper all over the place. The next job was learning how to make casts and pour "pigs" out of very hot lead. The next thing I learned was to feed the printing press. I would climb about four feet up in a platform and feed the paper into the printing press. The size of the print paper was about 4 feet by 8 feet. If you messed up or the clippers did get the paper, the paper would roll all up in the rollers which had the ink. It was a mess. It would take several minutes to clean up the shredded paper and to start again.

At the newspaper, Russell Grimes and Wayne Moore taught me how to make up advertisements and operate the lino-type. The saw and slugs were used to "justify" the advertisements. Wording was either set on the linotype or words were spelled out individually with letters from a printing case. There were many different sizes of letters. They could be as small as fourteen point or as large at seventy-two picas or larger. The most difficult ads that I worked on were the grocery store advertisements. They were usually a full page in the newspaper and it took a long time to put it together.

After the advertisements were formed, then they were placed in a rectangular frame made of steel, the size of one individual reading page in the newspaper. Around the advertisements were the news. These big squares when full with ads and news, 4 at a time were placed on the printing press. After the printing, the forms were taken off and they needed to be "Killed;" that is everything disassembled, the letters put back in their proper cases, and the lead was melted for it to be used again. After the newspaper was printed, then it needed to be folded and taken around town to different places. We also had a mailing machine which was used to address the individual newspapers that went out of town. Besides doing the regular newspaper, we also did different kinds of printing jobs such as letterheads, envelopes, bank checks, school forms, etc. One exciting thing I remember is that on the early days that we went to work real early, Troy Martin would take us to a local restaurant to eat breakfast! Man that was really something else! I liked that very much!

Later on as I learned different things in the printing business, my boss asked me to cover a couple of our local football games. That was exciting and fun! It was a thrilled to see my "by line name" on the football story in the newspaper.

Experiencing Racism

I will share a sad story that happened to me as I was working for *The Olton Enterprise*. Once our football team, The Olton Mustangs, was playing a bi-district game out of town and my boss, Troy Martin, asked me to cover it. I remember I was running the side lines; I did not like to be in the press box. Our team was not very numerous as we only had four extra players to substitute. We lost badly! So, I was already disappointed, mad, and sad.

After the game, my girlfriend and I went to eat in a local restaurant. Well, it was full and we kept on waiting and waiting and no service. Finally, I got the attention of the waitress, and she told me, "I am sorry; Sir, but we do not serve Mexicans." I was hurt, embarrassed, and mad. I asked to see the manager, but the answer was, "He is not here!" It is sad that things like that happened in America, but they did.

In high school I did not socialize much with my classmates. I was too busy going to school and working. Once in a while I might go to a Friday football game. I remember going to perhaps one or two birthdays parties that my classmates invited me.

I will always remember that one Friday my Dad and I drove to Littlefield for a football game. He would not let me go by myself, so I said, "Well, Dad, why don't you go with me?" And he did. That was really something special for me. I believe that was the only time my Dad attended a football game.

At that time in history it was also not customary for Whites and Mexican to mix such as dating. Many years after graduation, one of my classmates told me that one of our teachers had asked all the boys on a trip to be taken by seniors, if they had any problems in rooming with me. All of them supposedly said no. As it turns out, I was unable to go on our senior trip. I could not afford it.

For several years I worked in *The Olton Enterprise*. After graduation from high school, I worked two years full time. I believe my salary was either $50 or $60 per week. As a freshman in high school I started working at 45c an hour; later I got a raise to 50c per hour. Wow! Troy Martin, my boss, sure wanted me to go to college but I was not sure. At that time I had a girlfriend and was not thinking about college.

Bro. Godsey also wrote a column in Spanish for *The Olton Enterprise*. Most of the news were related to the Hispanic people in town.

Growing up in a large family

Large families in America seem out of style. Perhaps the biggest reason involves economics. Parents say, "We don't know how to feed, clothe or educate more than two." In addition, we live in a troubled world, and the American family experiences many problems with children. Parents say, "We can handle only one or two children."

Some couples have even chosen not to have any children at all. And many couples don't stay married long enough to have more than one or two children. I don't know if my parents ever discussed the pros and cons of a large family. But if they had stopped after five children, I would not exist.

In the Biblical times we have many examples of large families. If families had stopped at four or five, we would never have had great men like King David or Joseph.

My parents remained married for more than fifty years when Dad died in 1985. I don't know how they managed, but they raised fourteen children. Four died at a very early age. So I grew up with seven sisters and two brothers.

In the past ten years we have lost my oldest brother, Richard; and two sisters, Rachel and Julia. Rachel was the baby of the family.

Let me share a few things about my seven sisters. From the youngest to the oldest they include: Raquel, Irene, Sara, Martha, Luisa, Julia and Margarita. First, let me make some points about them. They are all beautiful women, and very smart. They have always worked hard and are followers of Jesus Christ.

Martha and Luisa were born in Monterrey, Mexico, so they often took a lot of kidding about being illegal aliens. And, around our families, we often referred to them as *panzas mojadas*—the Spanish equivalent of "wetbacks." After they married, the process of naturalization took them a long time. Our government really gave Luisa a very hard time. By 1980, two of her children had already graduated from high school in Cuero, and the authorities still refused her citizenship even though our family had lived in Texas since 1946. Martha, married a military man, has travelled all around the world. She has lived in Hawaii, Alaska and Germany. She also lived in Abilene long enough to earn a degree from Hardin-Simmons University.

Margarita and Julia married first. They both married Baptist ministers. As the oldest, Margarita always had more responsibility around the family. When Mother came to Texas from Mexico to work, Margarita took charge of the family. She did all the cooking, cleaning, washing. Margarita also washed and ironed my clothes during my first two years in college.

Margarita has the record for the number of husbands! Her first husband, the Rev. Milton Martinez, died of pneumonia. Cancer took the second one, the Rev. Bernabe Romero. Many family members felt it their responsibility to let third hubby the Rev. Robert Greaves know that Margarita had the record for burying husbands.

Mother assigned Julia many times to make the flour tortillas at home. My oldest brother and I loved to sneak into the kitchen and grab a freshly made tortilla and then run for our lives out of the house. She never caught us. Nothing compares to a homemade tortilla, and Julia could roll out some of the best.

Irene spent a couple of nights behind bars. In jail, the first thing she did was ask for a broom to sweep the place up. Irene, thirteen, had decided to marry her boyfriend, and Mom and Dad did not approve. When they refused, Irene eloped and Dad had both of them put in jail. Later, my parents permitted Irene and Mario to marry, and after forty-five years they remain happily married. Mario has often said, "If it weren't for Irene, we wouldn't have the things we have." They have owned their own fence company for more than twenty years in Garland. They have paid for their huge home, which has a swimming pool and a basketball court in the backyard.

Sarah, as a single parent, worked her way through school. She received a Bachelor's degree from Hardin-Simmons University, and has taught school for many years. Sarah has survived a knee and hip transplant. She has suffered with arthritis but she is a tough cookie!

The baby of the family is Rachel. She has earned a bachelor's and a master's degree from HSU. She tells me I used to "give noogies" to her and Irene on the head and made them kneel in a corner when they misbehaved. (Naturally, I don't remember that!) Lately, she has shown much courage fighting leukemia. Two months ago, she received a bone marrow transplant, and is on her way to recovery. Sister Martha gladly donated the bone marrow. Rachel did pass away on December 28, 1993. She fought the good fight.

I have had the privilege of having three of my sisters as my students. I taught Rachel at Abilene High School and at HSU. Julia and Sarah have also taken my classes at HSU. I must say they performed as model students and certainly behaved in class.

All of my living sisters are great grandmothers. So often in conversation the talks changes to grandchildren.

Now, let me tell you some things about my older and younger brother. Both Richard (Rico) and Samuel (Sammy) were tough "hombres." In school Rico was involved in several fights. Sammy was a U.S. Marine. Rico got a job driving a tractor at age 14 or 15. He was always a good worker. Both Rico and Sammy were good mechanics. They taught me a lot on that subject.

I have shared only but a few sweet memories from our large family. We struggled financially at times, and we never owned a new car or a new house, but we survived. And I don't remember ever missing a meal. I believe our struggles and challenges in the family helped us all to cope better in the outside world.

My College Days

It was my brother-in-law, the Rev. Milton Martinez, husband of my sister Mague who encouraged me to go to school. One day he told me: "Joe, one of these days you and others are going to apply for a certain job, and the one who has the college degree will probably get the job." He also said, "You are always telling the Hispanic young people that they need to continue their education. You need to be an example to them." Milton literally took me by my hand and brought me from Olton, Texas to Abilene, Texas where Hardin-Simmons was located. I nearly changed my mind about coming to Hardin-Simmons because of the weather. That day that we came to Abilene it was very hot and humid!!! Olton is very dry compared to the humidity in Abilene.

The First Baptist Church of Olton, Texas, gave me an offering of $300.00 for college use. The Women Missionary Union through the Mary Hill Davis annual offering provided a college scholarship of $2,000 for Baptist Latin American students. To qualify for the scholarship you had to be a member of a Baptist Spanish speaking church, and be recommended by your minister. In high school, you had to have an average of a B. When I started school at Hardin-Simmons, the tuition was $14.00 per hour. I am very happy and proud to say that when I graduated from HSU, I did not own anything. Praise the Lord!

My freshman or sophomore year I was drafted into the military and reported for a physical exam in Abilene. But, because I was enrolled in school, I was deferred from serving at that time. I did enjoy the two years that I was enrolled in HSU's Reserve Officers Training Corp. I learned a lot.

Milton helped to enroll me at HSU and also helped me in finding a job. He and my sister Mague encouraged me a lot. They would come and take me to the movies, and out to eat. Mague would wash and iron my clothes while I attended HSU. At that time Milton was pastor of a Baptist mission in Merkel, Texas, near Abilene.

I had no idea about college life! My parents had not attended college at all. I had not known anyone who had attended college, nor had I ever visited in a college. Milton helped me to sign up for 14 hours. My scores on the SAT indicated that I needed help with English. Because of my scores the English teachers signed me up for college English which met every day. This class was for students who needed extra help in English. I went and told the head of the English Department, Mrs. Lacy, that I could not take English every day that I was going to have to work to support myself. Mrs. Lacy was very kind and she said: "Young man, go to that desk and write me a page on why you came to college." I did. After looking at my paper she said: "I believe you can handle a regular English class." And, I did!

All male students had to sign up for Reserve Officers Training Corp (ROTC). We wore our full Army military clothes on Wednesdays and Fridays when we marched. Military classes were on Monday, Wednesday, and Friday. Once or twice a month we went to the rifle range. I was not too bad! At HSU I had no idea what I was going to major or minor in. At one point I decided that I wanted to be a teacher and that I would major in mathematics. I changed my mind really quickly one summer when I took Calculus. I went to class every day and I even had a tutor but it did not take. I made a big fat "F" in that class. My only F in college!

My Spanish teacher, Mrs. Lunn Rodgers, liked me and one day she told me, "Joe, I want you to finish college and go get a Ph.D.!" I said to myself, "Lady, I am having trouble passing college classes, and you want me to do what?" Evidently she saw something in me that I had not seen. She was a tough teacher and expected a lot from us.

I did not have much time to study as I began working nearly full time off campus at Russey's Print Shop. Every day I had classes in the morning, and at 1:00 p.m. I would go to work. Many times I worked 40 hours a week. I began working at Russey's for $1.25 an hour. My main job was setting type in the linotype for printing jobs we did in the shop. I also ran a small printing press called "The Little Giant." I remember my first big and long job was printing the 1960 presidential ballots for Taylor County. I believe we printed over 50,000 ballots! It was a large ballot, probably, 14 inches by 18 inches.

The owner of Russey's Printing Shop was Mr. D.P. Russey and his wife. The one that really ran the shop was his son, Joe Russey, a HSU graduate. Many times there was a big conflict on how to do things between father and son. I sometimes was in the middle of things. Mr. D.P. would tell me to do something and then Joe would come and tell me something different. There was a lot of conflict between father and son. The older Mr. Russey did not like to spend money on equipment or parts for the machinery we had. Something, Joe and I ordered some needed things behind Mr. Russey's back.

While at HSU it was also Milton who took me to my first Dallas Cowboy game in the Cotton Bowl in Dallas, Texas. The tickets were $3.00!!! I remember Calvin Hill, a rookie running back who gave us a big a show.

The first two Hispanics who I met at HSU were Carmen Perez and Tim Villasana. They both were friendly and made me feel at home. Later other Hispanic students came such as Filemon Ortiz, his brother Abel Ortiz, Rebecca Ramirez, Martha Villalobos, Luisa Villalobos, Rebecca Alvarez, and George Mota.

My first year I stayed in Ferguson Dorm. My roommate was Kenneth Hoover. He left at the end of the semester. It was not until recent that we had communication again. Kenneth married and has three adult children.

In HSU I attended our famous national Rodeo. Many schools out of state came in for the competion. I attended all the HSU Cowboy football games at home. We did not win any. The last game I saw was at Shotwell Stadium and that game ended in a fight. We were playing Trinity from San Antonio. At that time we had a losing streak of 28 games. Our Quarterback was Hayseed Stephens and our No. 2 QB was Freddie Martinez who had helped Abilene High School win state in football.

How I Met Liandra in Abilene

When I came to Hardin-Simmons, I had a scholarship called The Latin American Scholarship given by Texas Women's Missionary Union through the annual Mary Hill David Offering. One requirement of that scholarship was that I had to attend an Anglo Baptist church for one year. I was attending University Baptist Church because it was close to the university. One Sunday when we got out of church and I was in the car I saw three girls walking together in the direction of the nurses dormitory which was close to the church. The girls had walked from their nurse's dorm to the church. The one in the middle had long black hair and she was Mexican-American.

The other time I saw Liandra was when I went to Hendrick Hospital to see a friend of ours, Maria Loya. As we were going down to her room, I noticed this real pretty tall Mexican-American girl, and I knew this was the same girl I had seen in church. She was behind the desk; she seemed to be filling out papers or cards. As we walked out of Maria's room I went back and asked Maria to find out the name of the Mexican-American nurse. Maria and her husband Joe laughed and they said that they would try.

I knew the nurses attended classes at H-SU, especially in the chemistry department. I wasn't taking chemistry but my roommate, Kenneth, was. I told him to look around and find out about a Spanish girl with long black hair and that she was fairly tall. Well, it happened that he was sitting in front of Helen Hurtado from the nurses' dorm in chemistry class and he couldn't figure out if that was the girl I was talking about or even if she was a Spanish girl. I told him he had the wrong girl when he told me she was short and not too pretty, but much later, he got courage enough to ask for information about Liandra. He was told that there was a Spanish girl in the nurses dorm, tall, black hair and that everybody called her "Lonnie"—her real name was Liandra Olivares. Some girls had problems with the pronunciation of "Liandra," so they tagged her with "Lonnie."

I called this young lady, who I had never met, at the nurses' dorm and asked if she wanted to go with me to the movies. Well, as luck would have it, she already had a date for that weekend. I always have plan B ready, so I asked, "Well, how about next weekend?" To my surprise she said, "Yes."

I had gone to the nurses' dorm one or two times before, to see a friend of Kenneth from Colorado City, but at that time I still didn't know Liandra's name. That Sunday I was all nervous and didn't know what to do. I was pretty excited as I went in and asked at the desk for Lonnie and I was hoping they knew her last name or not to ask me because I sure didn't know it! Well, they buzzed her room and they told me she would be right down. I walked down to the waiting room and looked at the newspaper, but all that time I was thinking, I hope I have the girl I want. I said to myself what if this is not the girl I had seen two times before; maybe she was big, fat and ugly or just not the girl I would want to go out with. I was wearing my black suit with white spots as I sat back to relax in the sofa, Liandra came out. I did not get up real soon to meet her because I wanted to be sure that she was my date, I waited till she made the first move. She went and put her card out at the desk, and then she turned to me . . . smiled, and said, "Are you ready?" Boy, then I was for sure that she was the right one, and wow, was she beautiful! She was dressed very pretty. She was probably the one that received the shock about me and not me about her.

The young people supper dining room at University Baptist was real pretty decorated with sorts of Christmas goodies, and pretty dim lighting. After church, we went down to Rip's for a Coke. I did not know what to talk about because I did not know anything about her only that she was in nursing school—well, that was enough, because I asked her to tell me about nursing; believe me, she did a nice job of it. And then we got to talking about sick people in general, especially the Mexican-American people. That night, I learned that she had a big love in her heart for the Mexican-American people, especially those that did not have the money to pay the doctor, medicine, or hospital. After our date that night, I saw her the following week; then the following two weeks I went home. I sent her a Christmas card, but she probably didn't get it as I didn't know her correct name, yet, and I just sent it in care of Hendrick Hospital.

Well, I fell in love with Liandra on our first date. But . . . . I was sad to learn that she had a boyfriend who was in the military . . . ugh! She also talked about graduating from nursing school and joining the Navy. Strike two!! Well, we started going out together. I think it was one day during the week that I called her and we went out for a Coke. We were in front of "Mickey's," a drive-in restaurant near HSU. I was just talking away when she said, "I don't know if you know but I need to be in the dorm by 10 p.m." Well, I quickly started up the car and drove her to the dorm. This story is just to tell people out there that "once upon a time" there were curfews for girls!!!

We started dating, but I still had other commitments with another girl, and when Liandra was nominated and elected Valentine sweetheart for the school of nursing I could not accompany her. I was out of town. Today, I could kick myself.

Another time we had a conflict because I have never danced in my life and she either asked me or told me she was going to a dance. Well, I probably did not pay attention because the dance was part of the celebration of her brother Jesse's wedding. Later when I find out about it, I felt bad.

Liandra and I became officially boyfriend, girlfriend on a Wednesday, March 8, 1961. She gave me a picture 5 X 7 with a nurse uniform on March 24, 1961. On May 13, 1961, Liandra and I took off to meet my parents and family in Olton, Texas. Something happened to my car in Merkel, and we didn't leave until 8:30 p.m. that night. We arrived in Olton around midnight. I think Liandra slept with Luisa and Martha. The next morning we went to church; and we returned to Abilene in the afternoon. Liandra liked Daddy—she told me so—she was well pleased with my family.

One funny thing happened at Will Hair Park near Hardin-Simmons. A policeman came to our car and asked Liandra for identification. He thought Liandra was a "run-away." He apologized and said, "I don't think you fit the description young lady."

A Member of The Abilene Downtown Rotary Club

In 1980, I was invited to become a member of The Abilene Downtown Rotary Club. Our Rotary Club in Abilene started in 1926. I was nervous and excited and did not know what to expect. I knew a few of the men because I had met them while I served as a councilman for the city. There were also a few Hardin-Simmons professors who were members. Charles Garraway was the Rotarian who proposed me for membership. The way I qualified was that I was chairman of the HSU Foreign Language Department.

The Rotary club had been started in Chicago in 1905 for businessmen to have fellowship with other business men. Today Rotary International is all around the world and membership is into the millions.

Our Rotary club meets every Friday at noon. We start with a meal and then the program. The program begins with a prayer, and then we sing the National Anthem and say the pledge to the American flag. Guests are introduced and then there are announcements. There is a chairman of the day who introduces the speaker or program. I have enjoyed the many programs we have had.

Here are a few of the hundreds of programs I have seen at Rotary: the local mayor or city manager to give a report on the city; different singing groups from the three colleges; many CEOs from nonprofit organization; exchange students speaking about their countries; foreign business men and women talking about their countries.

The last three years we have enjoyed putting "Taste of Abilene" as a local fund raiser. We invite the Abilene Restaurant Association to come to the Civic Center and give out samples of their fine food. We sell tickets for $30 each. We have cleared from $12,000 to $22,000. This money is given away to local needed non-profit organizations. A grant's committees received applications and from $500 to $2,000 are given to each needed organization. This year (2010) the following organizations received funds: Noah Project, Boys Ranch and Literacy Council.

Our club also participates in helping the local Salvation Army ring the bell during the Christmas holidays to raise funds.

Rotary does so many good things. Rotary International awards scholarship for students to study abroad. Two of my students at HSU have received these scholarships: Laura Moore and Martin Cuellar. Laura continued her studies in English in London; and Martin studied piano in Barcelona, Spain. We also participated in student exchange programs. We have been blessed through the years to have had foreign students to come to our three local high schools: Wylie, Cooper, and Abilene. Business men and women from other countries have also travelled and visited our town and other towns to find out how things work in America.

. . . And every year Rotary International has a beautiful float in the Annual Rose Party in Pasadena, California. Our local club always contributes for this float.

Our Rotary motto is: **"Service above self."**

As Rotarians we try to live everyday by **"The Four-Way Test":** As anyone can see, these are good questions as check points in a person's everyday living and treatment of others:

First, is it the Truth?
Second, Is it Fair to all concerned?
Third, Will it build Goodwill and Better Friendships?
Fourth, Will it be beneficial to all concerned?

In 1994 I served as president which was very exciting. That year we had around 165 members. As president-elect I attended the International Rotary convention in Taipei, Taiwan. It was exciting and scary. It was good to rub shoulders and meet with Rotarians from other parts of the world. Another year Liandra and I attended the RI Convention which was held in Mexico City. It was very exciting. My daughter Cecilia and her husband Roy were able to attend with us. That year I served as president, Mrs. Myra Rainey was our Executive Director. She did a great job.

My last Friday to serve as president, the incoming president Paul Lenker surprised me and invited a local Folkloric dance team to perform in my honor. I was also very honored as some Rotarians made it possible for me to become a "Paul Harris Fellow." To be a Paul Harris Fellow, a person has to give $1,000 to Rotary International. I had been a sustaining fellow and needed only a few hundred dollars to become a Paul Harris Fellow.

That day, U.S. Congressman Charles Stenholm was visiting with our club and he got to dance with one of the young ladies.

I have met and made many friends in Rotary; some come and go and some stay for a while. Some of who I consider my friends are Fred Lee Hughes, Bob Kuykendall, Barbara Rollins, David Stubbeman (deceased), Paul Lenker, J.T. Box, Bob Hunter, Betty Hukill, Orval Philbeck (deceased),

George Dawson (our family physician), Peter Agnell, Morris Baker, Bruce Bixby, Raymond Blasingame, Tom Boecking, Dave Boyll, Ralph Bridwell, Ed Brokaw, Turner Cariker, Malcolm Coco, C.G. Gray, John Harris, Spike Harris, Paul Johnson, Mary Beth Kilgore, Austin King, Charlie Kitchell, Bruce Lampert, Peggy Manning, Jack North, Randy Piersall, Marty Pothier, Wes Ratliff, Buzz Rehm, B.C. Roberson, Mike Schweikhard, Bob Test, Jim Tredennick, Tim Yandell, and Kayla Christianson. I am very proud to be a Rotarian!!! I very much enjoy the fellowship and the camaraderie of the men and women.

My First Teaching Assignment

I have always said that God has a sense of humor. When I graduated from HSU, I wanted so much to get a teaching job in Abilene where my wife was a nurse at Hendrick Hospital and we were pretty much settled at our church, Ambler Baptist Church. I had put out several teaching applications.

I was feeling down because an administrator at HSU, had told me, "Joe, you need to apply in South Texas because no one is going to hire you here in the north part of Texas." (He meant no one would hire a "Mexican" in Abilene or north of it.)

Well, I believe it was on a Monday afternoon that I signed my teaching contract with Brownwood Independent School District. Believe it or not, the next morning around 7:30 a.m. the principal of Lincoln Junior High in Abilene called me at home and offered me a job. Oh, how I wanted to say yes, but I have always been a man of my word. I told him, "I am sorry Sir, but I signed a contract last night in Brownwood."

I had a lot of fun teaching the seventh and eighth grade students at Brownwood Junior High. My homeroom was a class of 7th graders. In those days a teacher could still use the paddle for discipline if needed. So, all during the year for one reason or other I had used the paddle on all of the boys except one. In May, the students told me that I had spanked everyone except so and so. Well, I said, we cannot have that. So, I asked the young student to come to the front and I gave him three licks. He was a good sport.

My wife did not like Brownwood. All of our friends were in Abilene! We joined La Primera Iglesia Bautista Mexicana (First Mexican Baptist Church) in Brownwood where Rev. Jose Rivas was the pastor. We loved his preaching and teaching. He was a wonderful man. He and his wife took us in. But . . . the church members were a lot older than we were, so we could not relate to them. No church member ever visited us in our home.

But God always uses circumstances to teach his children. Liandra and I grew closer to each other. We watched a lot of TV together. We enjoyed watching the old Western movies. During the year she became pregnant with our oldest daughter, Cecilia. We were poor, poor! My salary was $3,700 per year. That friends, is around $300 per month! On pay day, we would splurge and go to the Dairy Mart for an ice cream cone.

I am sorry to say and to the regret of my wife, we had to sell a very old Singer sewing machine that was given to my wife from her grandmother. We also cashed in several books of green stamps that we have saved. In those days, business people gave you green stamps that you could redeem at a later date. We lived about two miles out of town in a small rented brick house. When we needed to mow the yard, we borrowed the Rivas electric mower.

While we were living in Brownwood, one afternoon, Liandra's two sisters, Benita and Mary and their spouses, Fred and Jimmy came to visit us. After they left, we were happily surprised that they had bought us groceries and stored them in our kitchen cabinets without us knowing! God always provides!

After school was out in May, Liandra and I moved back to Abilene for the summer so I could work part time for The Pender Company as a linotype operator and a printer. Well, again, believe it or not but one summer day I received a call from the Spanish teacher Mrs. McElroy at Abilene High where I had student-taught. She said, "Joe, I am going to resign as a teacher, do you want the job?" My question to her was, "Mrs. McElroy, do you think I can handle high school students?" She responded with great encouragement: "Of course you can, you will be a great teacher!" That afternoon, Mr. Fields, personnel director called me at home and offered me the job. I had a very hard time resigning in Brownwood because they had given me my first opportunity to teach, and then I had to tell Bro. Rivas that I was leaving Brownwood. Oh, that was very hard.

Two other good things happened while we lived in Brownwood. Three years later I returned to take night classes at Howard Payne College to begin working on my Master's degree. Liandra and I and our daughter Cecilia spent two summers in Brownwood so I could complete my degree.

The second good thing that happened was finding a 1941 Chevy. One day as we were driving around, I saw this 1941 black Chevrolet—just like the one Daddy used to drive back in the 50s in Sweetwater. It brought back a lot of good memories. I was able to buy that car—cash—for $125.00. For a long time, we used the 41 Chevy as our second car. I drove it, and other family members drove it. I remember, Jimmy Smith, Sarah Smith, and Gene Smith driving the car to Hardin-Simmons. Cecilia, my daughter, and Angie Gutierrez, my niece were not too fond of my 1941 Chevrolet. At times, I would drive to Mann Middle School to pick the girls and they would hide so they would not have to ride in the car!! I remember my poor Mother trying to explain to the girls: "Listen, girls, people know that your Dad/uncle (me) has another car." Later in the 1980's Mr. Raul Castillo painted the 1941 Chevrolet and it looked like a new one. I believe Mr. Castillo only charged me for the paint. I believe I paid him $300.00.

An Eagle at Abilene High School, 1965-1971

My first year teaching at Abilene High School was in the Fall of 1965. I had five classes plus supervising a big study hall (with about 100 students) during the last period of the day. I had a great time teaching in high school. I never had discipline problems in my classes. I found out that the good students are the ones who usually take a foreign language. Within a year or two I became head of the department. The other Spanish teacher was Miss Lynda Collins. Sally Jones taught French; and Mrs. Mary Griffith taught German.

Our school principal was Mr. Escoe Webb. He ran the school with "an iron hand." You did not mess around with him. He seldom smiled; but he was a good man. Every year when it was time to ask teachers to contribute to the United Way, he would tell us teachers, "If you are only going to give one dollar, don't, I will give it for your!" We got the message. Another thing he enjoyed doing was throwing a piece of paper on the floor in that big study hall when we had faculty meetings. After he started the meeting, he would say, "Well, I see no one picked up that piece of paper on the floor. I guess that is not your job!"

Mr. Harold Brinson was our assistant principal, and he was also very tough. One time he asked me to be a witness as he paddled two boys. We went down to the boiler room, and he asked the boys to take everything from their back pockets, and then he asked that each one lean forward holding on to a post; he gave them three hard licks! He then would shake their hands and say, "I don't want to see you here again." Not many came back for seconds!

Mrs. Ellen Turner, a Senior English teacher, taught across my room, number 211. I learned a lot from her. Once she told me, "Mr. Alcorta, don't raise your voice when you teach, make the students listen to you." Her students really respected her. Later our paths crossed again as she taught English part time at HSU.

I was also part of history at Abilene High! Bad, I guess! One day, I was informed that most of the Hispanic students had walked out of classes. At that time I did not know why or what had happened. I did know the two Hispanic leaders who had led the walk-out. I went to Sears Park where the students were meeting and I told them the best thing for them to do was to return to the classroom. I promised that I would try to help. I believe that the students were told that they were receiving "zeroes" for all assignments not turned in! After three days the students returned to class.

I have to be honest and say that there has always been discrimination in the public schools. You can make all kinds of laws, but you cannot change people with laws. And there will continue to be discrimination until Jesus returns. Remember, in Sweetwater I went to Emiliano Carranza because I could not attend with the whites. Once an Anglo teacher within my hearing ears told another teacher: "I would never permit my daughter to date a Mexican or even to go on a double date with a Mexican couple." The same teacher later said, "I don't know why the Mexicans don't like me."

I believe it was during my second year at AHS (1966-67) that Blacks from Woodson High School had a choice to come over to AHS or remain at the all-Black school. Gradually all students would have to come to AHS. Many Black students came to AHS. I remember hearing a white teacher say, "God help us all!"

I remember one Friday night when I was working a basketball game; there was a big commotion and a lot of talk because a Black football player had walked in with a white girl into the basketball game. Today no one blinks an eye. Mixed dating and marriage is accepted. There are many mixed couples dating and marrying. In our own family we have had two Blacks to marry two Hispanics; and several whites to marry Hispanics.

One great moment I remember in my life is when I was selected inspiration teacher of the year in sports. I still cherish that pen holder medal. That was great. To me, it was a great honor. Two students, Jaquetta and Dale nominated me. I was also honored that at one pep rally I got to give the pep talk to the football boys. We were going to play Midland Lee, and I told the boys that we were going to make "bulldog soup" out of the team as I pulled a soup bowl from a bag.

Another great time in high school was when my wife and family members helped me to put on a Mexican dinner in the school cafeteria as a fund raiser for students for a Mexico trip. It was fun. Many students sold the tickets for the Mexican dinner. The dinner was served between 5 and 7:00 p.m. We also had dessert for extra money. The dinner was a great success. The dinner was also to teach the students how to work. Not only did they have to sell tickets, but also to help prepare the food, serve the food, and then clean up! The AHS cafeteria ladies helped us a lot and some business people donated some supplies. A few of my pretty students showed up with pretty dresses and painted nails. I quickly told them, not everyone can take tickets, and someone has to wash dishes! Boy, they didn't like that! The money made from the dinner was equally divided among the students making the trip to Mexico.

One year our AHS Eagle school bus driver, Mr. Marshall, from Abilene drove us all from Abilene, Texas, to Monterrey, Nuevo Leon, Mexico. In Monterrey, he drove us up to Horsetail Falls! It was a great trip. I remember the sponsors were Mr. and Mrs. Larry Dooley, Cop and Susie Coppingers, head football Coach Jerry Thormalen and his wife.

It seems like every year we faced different challenges at the border crossing. One year they asked me, "Do you have written certified permission from parents for their son/daughter to go with you to Mexico?" No, I did not! Another time they asked, "Do you have a written certified permission for the driver to take this bus into Mexico?" No, I did not!

One year a black student, Chris, from Kenya went with us to Mexico. He was our star soccer player at HSU. At the border, they told us that Chris did not have the right document to go into Mexico. So, Chris, Frank (an older student with us), and I made a U-turn and tried to cross the border back to the U.S. Coming in they told us that Chris could not come in to the U.S. I told them, "Listen, we tried to go into Mexico and they have sent us back." Well after much discussion an official escorted us back across the U.S. I told Chris, "You go to the lawyer's office in the morning and get the right document and we will return tomorrow." We did return from Monterrey the next day and we crossed back into Mexico with Chris with no problems.

A few days later upon our return, at customs, they asked me and the students. "Is everyone an American citizen?" We all answered, "Yes!" Well, Chris told me from the back of the van, "Mr. Alcorta, I need to report every time I cross a border, if not, I will get in trouble." We tried to convince Chris to stay in the van but he kept on persisting. Sure, enough, as soon as we went in, the customs official, told him, "We are cancelling your passport right now and we are sending you back to Africa." It was shocking and scary. Chris knelt down crying and was begging that they not do that. I tried to counsel and settle Chris down. Then I asked the official: "Can we do anything?" They said, "Well, you can go before a judge on Monday morning and plead your case." I answered, "Yes, sir, we want to do that." So, Frank and I took Chris back to Laredo, Mexico and found him a motel room. We told him to stay put and that we would come back for him later.

It was funny, that the first thing the motel lady told us: "We do not admit girls into the room!" We said, "Do not worry; he does not have any money!" Well, we drove in to Abilene and very early on a Sunday morning I called Dr. Jesse Fletcher, Hardin-Simmons president, and told him that we had left HSU's star soccer in Mexico. He and another HSU official went for him on Monday. They took Chris' HSU files to prove that he indeed was a HSU student.

Another episode was a little different in Mexico City. We were shopping with Abilene High School students in a big popular store downtown Mexico City when students came to me and said, "Mr. Alcorta, they have one of our students," in the basement. It didn't sound good. Sure, enough, when I went the officers told me, "We caught your student shop lifting! We will have to take him downtown and book him." I quickly said, "How much will it take to not take this student downtown!" They gave me an amount and I paid it. As soon as we left the store, I told my student, "You owe me 500 pesos!" He paid me and apologized for doing that crazy thing. He had stolen a gold broche for his sister.

The trips to Mexico were memorable, but I also enjoyed the AHS sports. As a teacher, to earn a little extra money during the school year, I helped to take tickets, sell tickets, or direct traffic at baseball, basketball, and football games. We were paid $5.00 per game. Of course, I enjoyed watching the games free. That is when I started liking basketball and baseball. I grew up loving football.

The only thing I did not like at AHS was that those six years I taught we always had a losing football season. One year we had two recent graduates of the University of Texas as coaches. They did not last long. The coach told me they were just "re-building."

Basketball was a little different. Two or three years we won our district and went to the playoffs. I enjoyed watching the run and shoot of our team. Every time we played Hobbs, New Mexico, the score would be over 100 points. Nat Gleaton and Harold Wilder were the coaches. One year we made it to state. Liandra and I were blessed that we could attend that tournament. We played our first game on Friday which we lost; and then we played the consolation game on Saturday.

AHS played an important role to my family. All of our four children graduated from Abilene High. All four children had good teachers. Cecilia graduated in 1983; Joe in 1987; Adriel in 1994, and Andrew in 1998. In middle school all three boys played football and basketball. In high school Joe played some football and three years in baseball; Andrew played basketball; and Adriel was in gymnastics and also played in the band. In academics Joe graduated number 11 in his high school class of class of 441 graduating seniors, made the National Society, and received a Presidential Scholarship for Texas A&M.

I was also proud that my Dad was part of the team at AHS as he worked as a custodian for several years. His shift was from 3:00 p.m. to 11:00 p.m.

A year or two I actually drove my 1941 black Chevy to AHS. It was our second car. I remember one year that one of my students, Sarah Skiles and a friend ran up at the faculty park lot and jokily said, "Hey Clyde, where is Bonnie?" (Bonnie and Clyde were famous gangsters in a movie) Those were the good ole days! I did not know at that time, but in the future, Sarah's Dad, Dr. Elwin Skiles was to be my president and boss at Hardin-Simmons. In 2005, Dr. Skiles was honored to have a building on campus named after him.

When I was teaching at AHS, I met Margaret Robbins, another Spanish teacher. She left AHS to go teach at Hardin-Simmons. When she left, I told her: "Margaret, don't forget about me."

A Cowboy at Hardin-Simmons University, 1971-till the Present

Well, believe it or not, but Margaret Robbins husband got a transfer with his job to Brownwood, Texas, and Margaret resigned at HSU. She called and told me, "Joe, you need to apply to teach Spanish here at Hardin-Simmons. I am leaving." I did not do it. I was very happy at AHS.

God works in mysterious ways! Dr. Ray Ellis, chairman of Humanities at HSU, came to our home one afternoon and asked if I wanted to teach at HSU. I was a little scare but after praying about it, I agreed to meet with Dr. Elwin Skiles on a Saturday morning at HSU.

One of the first things Dr. Skiles told me: "Joe, if you come and teach here at HSU, you are going to have to take a cut in pay!" And, I did. My new title was, "Instructor in Spanish." With time I was given tenure; and then promoted to Assistant, Associate, and Full Professor. Remember, I started making $3,700 a year at Brownwood. I probably left AHS, making a little over $5,000 annually. So, you can get an idea what I was making at Hardin-Simmons!

Of course at that time (1971) I did not even dream that one of my children (Cecilia) would one day use the family benefit plan offered by HSU and get her college education free. Our oldest son, Joe, also benefitted some from the family benefit plan as he took a couple of courses in the summer while he attended Texas A&M.

My first classes that I taught at Hardin-Simmons were in the Fall of 1971. At that time professors were teaching 15 hours or 5 classes. Soon after I came aboard, the faculty convinced the administration to drop the teaching load from 15 to 12 hours. After I became the head of The Foreign

Language Department, you were paid extra for three semester hours. If possible and feasible, a head department could teach only nine hours.

Very soon I fell in love teaching at Hardin-Simmons. If you do your job right, literally nobody bothers you. Oh, yes, you have forms, reports, and grades, and faculty meetings to attend, but that is everywhere. We also have office hours where it is expected for you to be in the office if a student needs you. At present we are to be available ten hours a week.

When I came to HSU, all students were required to sign up for a foreign language. The languages offered were French, German, and Spanish. Greek was offered by the Bible Department. Because foreign languages were required we normally had large classes in all the languages. And we also had several teachers. Today, languages are no longer required for everybody. The students who are working on a Bachelor of Arts degree are required to take twelve hours. Other fields such as music require only three hours; sociology requires twelve hours; and criminal justice twelve. With these changes we have lost teachers and students. However, despite the changes, in most years, Spanish has been the popular language.

Our classes use to be made up of about twenty-five or thirty students. When I started teaching we offered a major and minor in French, German, and Spanish. Today that is no longer true. We no longer teach French, and our German classes are very small.

Through the years my popular classes have been Elementary and Intermediate Spanish. Since we are a small school, we switch out in teaching advanced courses such as Advanced Spanish Grammar, Linguistics, Conversational Spanish, Hispanic Civilization, and several Literature Courses. At present there are only two full time professors in Spanish—Dr. Teresia Taylor and myself. We have one part time person who teaches one Spanish class. Other professors who have come and gone through the years in our department have been: Dr. Don Whitmore, Dr. David Gifford, Dr. Jim Alvis, and Dr. Nancy Bundy.

Of all the professors above, Jim Alvis and I have been the closet. Jim and I attended many Texas Foreign Languages Associations meetings through the year. Jim and I also travelled in Mexico. Through the years Jim has enjoyed buying and selling antiques. Recently he came over to our house and gave Liandra a set of Depression dishes. Boy that was something!

I have enjoyed my forty years plus at HSU. I have a lot of fun teaching. I do not see it as work. I see it as an opportunity and a ministry to be with students and to encourage them and guide them in their Christian walk.

The youngest student I have taught was Crystal Coe from Malaysia, 17 years old; and the oldest was a summer student from Abilene Christian University at age 84! This jolly senior citizen needed my Spanish class for his music degree at Abilene Christian University.

On Mondays and Tuesdays we pray before starting the classes. I normally ask for three things: prayer request, to share a blessing, and if they have a Scripture they would like to share. I already have had former students to say that they really enjoyed those "prayer periods" before class. I have enjoyed counseling with many of my students out of class. They have felt confidence in sharing with me their personal problems. I have had the pleasure of praying with many of my students in my office. I have counseled with many single mothers and single fathers. We have prayed for many friends and family members of my students. It is good that my students have felt at ease in asking me to pray for all these kinds of different situations. I have also had the pleasure and joy of praying with several administrators in their offices. I have prayed with Dr. Lanny Hall, Dr. Craig Turner, Dr. Jesse Fletcher, and Dr. Tomas Briscoe. Of course my close friend Earl Garrett, who worked in human resources, and I often prayed in his office about many things.

For several years I would sponsor a Mexico trip with our HSU students. The idea of the five week trip is to expose students to some of the Mexican culture. We always encourage our students to stay with Mexican families so they would be forced to use the Spanish language. We normally would go to Monterrey or to Mexico City. Guadalupe Sandoval (now decease), a cousin, would help us to find homes for the students while we were in Mexico. Another big helper for me in Mexico was Jose Guerra. Larry and Jo Dooley (Abilene teachers) had met Jose and they "adopted" him as their son. Jose was an excellent guide and as he grew older, he continued helping us with many things. Jose now is educated, married, and runs a successful business in Monterrey.

In Monterrey, we would take the students to Cola de Caballo (Horsetail Falls), Santa Rosa, a nice restaurant, Las Grutas de Garcia (Caverns), "el Mercado," and to Saltillo, a well known educational center. In Mexico City we would go to Xochimilco (the floating gardens), the pyramids, attend the National Mexican Folkloric Ballet, attend a jai lai game, University of Mexico City, and attend a bullfight. In the last five years, Dr. Teresia Taylor has taken students to Spain. Our school has an agreement with the University of Salamanca where students can enroll in courses at the university and receive credit at HSU.

Another thing we have done every year is celebrate Foreign Language Week. The first full week of March is when emphasis is placed on learning a second language in the United States. One year to celebrate the FLW, I encouraged the students to put on a Spanish play in the HSU theatre. It was a great success. In fact, we put on two plays: La Mariposa Blanca and La Venda. Martin Cuellar was the leading star. I could not believe that my students memorized all those lines in Spanish!! In other years, we have gotten the community involved. Our local mayor has declared the first week of March as Foreign Language Week. Sometimes we would order a Spanish movie and show it free in the library. We normally had a good turnout.

With forty years of teaching at Hardin-Simmons, many of my students have graduated and are very successful in different fields. Some have kept in touch. Here is a partial list of former students and some of the things that they are doing: (all these students are a blessing and an encouragement to me!)

Anderson, Claudia Venegas—Claudia is an elementary school teacher for Abilene.

Austin, Pam—One of my first early students in Spanish. Pam taught Kindergarten for Pioneer Drive for over 20 years. She was Ashby's (my grandson) teacher in 2007.

Bridges, Becky and Debbie. Becky was an outstanding Spanish student. She now is certified as a counselor in the Dallas area. Debbie is a school principal in San Antonio. Debbie was one of our drill instructor in our Intensive Spanish classes here in our FL Department. Their parents, Julian and Carlota served as missionaries to college students in Mexico City.

Faircloth, Alisa—This year (2011), Ms. Faircloth is Ashby's 3rd grade teacher at Ortiz Elementary School in Abilene, Texas.

Cuellar, Martin—Martin came from Del Rio, Texas. He borrowed his brother's car to come to HSU. In San Angelo the car got hot and Martin had to decide to continue or return. He came. Martin was my office helper for several years. He helped me a great deal with The Dallas Cowboy book. Martin married another former student of mine, Lori Bagwell. Martin received a Rotary scholarship to continue his studies in piano in Barcelona, Spain. He returned and earned a Ph.D. in piano at The University of Texas. Currently he is a professor of piano in Kansas. Martin and Lori have two teenage boys.

Garza, Dolores—Dolores is a P.E. teacher at Ortiz Elementary. She teaches my grandson, Ashby.

Jackson, Kassia—Kassia was an outstanding student in my Spanish classes. She has now earned a Master's degree in English at HSU. Kassia is the person who has proofread and corrected my two recent books.

Johnson, Lance—Lance was a Spanish major and is currently a pastor of a Hispanic church in Denton. Lance helped me with computer work. He put in all Spanish punctuation in a book I translated. My hat is off to Lance for caring for his wife, Dianne (Wartelle) who was bed ridden for over 15 years. Dianne passed away about 5 years ago. Dianne was also in my classes.

Daniels, Michelle—Michelle is a Spanish teacher in Wylie. She recently received her Master's in counseling. I have also taught both of her daughters. Michelle has helped me during the summer with my classes when I had to be gone.

Mejia, Isaiah—Isaiah is a pastor in Las Vegas, Nevada. He was a drill instructor for us in our Intensive Spanish program at HSU. Isaiah and his wife have purchased a bed and breakfast restaurant in South Carolina.

Molina, Mary Helen Muñoz—Mary Helen has worked for the Abilene Independent School District as a teacher and as an administrator. We met her family while we worshipped at Ambler Baptist.

Melba Carbona—Melba was our HSU queen one year. Melba met her husband in Mexico City while she was a missionary. Melba works in Ft. Worth. Melba was a very close friend of my sister Rachel.

Munton, Dr. Dan—Dan is a local well known respected Sports Medical Doctor. He also helps out with our HSU football players. He has taken care of a running injury I had. Dan and I attend the same church. He and his wife have visited my Sunday school class.

Flores, Ysau—Ysau has worked for textbook publishing companies in San Antonio for a long time. I also taught Ysau at Abilene High. I have also taught one of his daughters. Ysau and I have dinner once or twice a year in San Antonio.

Mandaville, Sarah—Probably the best student who I have ever taught in my early years. Sarah and her husband from San Antonio have nine children!

Gonzales, Sylvia—a teacher in the Dallas area. Sylvia has been faithful in coming to our Hispanic homecomings for years.

Aycock, Angela and Amy—twins, both are elementary teachers at Wylie. I see them every Sunday at Beltway Park Baptist as they hand out bulletins in an entrance door.

Santiago, Zulema Aguirre—a teacher at Ortiz Elementary.

Santibañez, *Rachel Aguirre*—a teacher at Fannin Elementary School.

Ybarra, Yolanda—a teacher in Plainview, Texas. She has been active with our HSU Hispanic homecoming activities

Vásquez, Alex. Alex taught for a while at Abilene High School and then went to law school. He is now a lawyer for Wal Mart in Arkansas. His dad, Rev. Paul Vasquez was our pastor at Ambler Baptist Church.

Pogue, Jimmy and Laura—Jimmy is a teacher at Abilene Cooper High School; and his wife Laura is a college English teacher at Hardin-Simmons. Jimmy went with us to Mexico. I can still see Jimmy on that poor burro; Jimmy's feet were touching the ground!

Kirles, Jeremy—Jeremy is my music worship leader at Beltway Park Baptist Church.

Relatives In My Classroom

Smith, Jimmy, a former brother-in-law; received a commission in the Army through ROTC, and served several years in the military. Jimmy has been a teacher and a counselor in Abilene for many years.

Smith, Jimmy—is a son of Jimmy Smith and Sarah Alcorta. Jimmy has served as a youth minister at Allen, Texas, and is soon to receive his counselor's degree.

Castillo, Cecilia Alcorta and her husband **Raul Castillo.** Cecilia taught at Franklin Middle School; and presently she is teaching algebra at Cooper High School. She recently earned a counselor's degree from Sul Ross University. Roy has worked at Kmart and Lowe's. Roy and Cecilia have three boys: Roy, Michael, and Trey.

I taught three of my sisters at HSU: **Rachel Alcorta Smith, Sarah Alcorta Smith,** and **Julia Gloria.** Rachel and Sarah were elementary school teachers. Rachel died at an early age with leukemia. Julia lacked a few hours to graduate.

HSU Employees In My Classroom

I have also taught some students who stayed here at HSU and worked on campus. Some of these students are: **Travis Seekins** (technology); **Brenda Harris** (communications); **Meredith Aims** (Graduate school); Eddy (Maintence); **Debbie McFarland,** and **Rene Taylor** (recruitment).

In 2000 I took a summer sabbatical and travelled to Spain. My main purpose was to see, hear, and learn more about the Spanish culture in person. My highlight in Spain was visiting and walking through the home of Miguel de Cervantes which was built in the 1600.

Cooking Tamales and Pancakes

I have never been lazy or afraid of hard work. I normally do what has to be done. Of course, when we were home, Mother and my sisters would do most of the cooking. After I married and had children I began to cook some.

In our early years of marriage, I started helping my wife making tamales. We used to sell them on the weekend to help our budget. If I remember correctly, we started selling them at $1.00 per dozen, or was it $3.00? Anyhow, as time marched on and materials got more expensive, we went up on our price from $4.00 to $5.00 and now in the year 2011 we sell them for $7.00 a dozen. They are the best tamales in the world!

These last few years, when we do make tamales, my main job is to cut up the meat (beef and pork) and get it into a big pan to cook for about an hour. After it is cooked I grind the meat. With the broth I mix and prepare the dough (flour, salt, chili blend, shortening) to spread into the corn shuck. Spreading the dough into the shuck is a slow process. Step number two is to put the meat on the shuck with the dough. Liandra then places the tamales in a pan and stems them for about one hour. My wife is one of a kind in preparing the meat—it is delicious. Of course, another one of my jobs is that I am the "official taster!" Liandra always asks me, "Honey, please taste the meat for spices, salt, taste, etc." Man, I love that!!! We make a great team in the kitchen!

Christmas 2010 our daughter and her husband Roy and boys surprised us by coming over to our home to help with the tamales. Roy has often asked Cecilia to learn from her Mother. I enjoyed teaching them as we went through the steps. Our son, Adriel, was video-taping the tamales lessons. At that time we were making tamales for the annual Alcorta Christmas party. We have had so many compliments on our tamales. It is now a tradition on Christmas several families call and ask for us to make their tamales. Of course, we normally give many dozens away.

As far as I can remember, I have always made migas **(mee-gahs)** for our children. I learned it from my Mother. My recipe is to cut up some corn tortillas in small pieces and place them in a pan with a small amount of oil. I let the tortillas become a little brown and crisp, and then I add wieners (or pieces of ham). After a couple of minutes I add eggs and mix it. Sometimes I add cheese.

In our extended family, I have a great reputation with my **pancakes**! My wife will quickly say that the recipe really belongs to her oldest sister, Mary Burns. She is right, but now seldom do I look at the recipe while mixing the dough. At the annual Alcorta Christmas party I am expected to do the pancakes—I love it!!! Most family members enjoy them.

I certainly believe that practice makes perfect and with that I refer to my **carne guisada (Kar-neh guee-sah-dah).** In brief, carne guisada is cut-up meat with potatoes and gravy. My secret is in the spices. To make the gravy a little thick I add a teaspoon of flour; and for a little extra flavor I add a spoonful of peanut butter.

Another plate which I have improved with practice is **chicken and rice**. First, I boil the chicken without the skin. I put a little oil in a pan and place a cup of rice and brown it. I use the broth to cook the rice plus the added chicken. I love to make this, but I love to eat it more!!!

For **breakfast** I can quickly fix **eggs, bacon, sausage, chorizo (shoh-reh-zo), refried beans**, and **toast or flour tortillas**. The **flour tortillas** are still my challenge in rolling them and making them round!

Allow me to give you the recipe for making flour tortillas. I know lots of people who love them! I know only a few women who still make them. Most people don't bother and they buy them at the store. I normally put four cups of flour in a bowl with baking powder, salt, and Crisco; mix with warm water and let the dough set for a while. Roll pieces of dough into a small ball and then with a rolling pin spread it pretty thin. I put it on the grill and turn it once. We Mexican-Americans still pride in ourselves that we do not need a spoon or a fork to eat as we cut off small pieces of tortillas to make into a "spoon."

Lately I have made lots and lots of **French fries**. My grandson, Ashby who has lived with for nine years does not eat too many things, but he does love French fries. I peel two or three potatoes, slice them up and place them in a frying pan with cooking oil.

The Beginning of my Christian Life

I was blessed to have been brought up in a Christian home, and as far as I remember, our family always attended church. I don't remember exactly when I accepted the Lord as my Savior, but I know it happened in Sweetwater, Texas around 1950 when I was 12 years of age. We were attending this small Mexican mission in Sweetwater and it was during one of the home services that I went to the front and told the preacher that I wanted to repent from my sins and be saved. I had to be baptized at First Baptist Church because our little mission did not have a baptistery. Either Rev. Manuel Ortiz or Rev. Lester Vinson baptized me.

I remember the small mission in Sweetwater, and within a year or two, a new church was built. My Dad, Ricardo Alcorta, was my Sunday school teacher. At church we had to fill out our church envelopes and in each envelope we had to mark several things such as being on time, giving an offering, and studying the lesson. We also had a memory verse to learn every Sunday.

Misión Bautista la Trinidad, Olton, Texas

In 1952, we moved to Olton, Texas, and our family joined the small Mexican Baptist Mission where Rev. Glen E. Godsey was the pastor. From Bro. Glen and his wife Oralia we learned much about church work and the Christian life. Bro. Godsey was very strict. He believed in giving the tithe (10% of what you earn) to the church; and he believed that going to the movies was a sin! So, for 5 years or all the time he was our pastor I did not go to the movies. I respected him so much. I became Bro. Godsey's right hand man at the church. I was always around him. He used to drive a yellow school bus to pick up people and I was right there with him.

We had a lot of fun at the mission. We frequently had young people activities on Friday nights. We would play all kinds of games. Every month we had an associational meeting made up of several other churches. The church who took the most would get the attendance banner. We seldom lost. At our church we had the organizations of Sunbeams, Royal Ambassadors, Girls Auxiliaries, Youth, Women's Missionary Union, and Brotherhood. There was something for every church member. Mother helped Mrs. Godsey with all the children and women's activities.

On special occasions, we had special services. On Mother's Day we would recognize the oldest to the youngest mother. Sometimes the mothers would receive flowers or other special gifts. Bro. Godsey and Oralia would always sing a special song about mothers for that day. The song always made me cry! On Easter we would have a sunrise service at 5:00 a.m. We would compete as to who was going to be there the earliest! After the service we would enjoy a nice breakfast. On Christmas we had a Christmas play, and at the end of the program, we would give out little bags full of fruit and candy. The little brown bag had an orange, an apple, a few pieces of candy and pecans. As usual, Bro. Godsey would dress as Santa Claus.

In our youth meetings with other churches we had Bible drills. Of course, no one could beat me!!! I knew the books of the Bible backwards and forwards! The person leading the drill, would give you the book of the Bible, chapter and verse, and then would say something like, "go!" The first person to find the Scripture would take a step to the front and begin reading the verse.

We also participated in the January Bible studies. Bro. Godey was our teacher. The classes were Monday through Friday for 2 hours each. Bro. Godsey would test us on that particular book so we could get a certificate and credit. I remember one year he taught us the life of Paul. Oralia and I made the highest grades. Later, Bro. Godsey told us that the book on Paul was taught at the seminary level!!!! Boy, we were very proud of ourselves.

On Halloween, it was a tradition for Bro. Godsey to dress up like a woman. He wore a big wig and would use either towels or grapefruits for his front side!!! He was a hit! We played different games. We also had a big tub full of water with apples on the bottom. With our hands behind our backs, we would try to get the apples with our mouths.

Since the mission did not pay Bro. Godsey very much, he often did other odd jobs to make ends meet. One year he joined us in the cotton fields of Roscoe Thomas. We could not believe it, there he was with us at 5:00 a.m. in the morning!

It was in Olton that our family began to marry. The first to marry was Julia. She met her husband, the Rev. Patricio Gloria in a church meeting. Bro. Godsey married them in 1952. Pat and Julia left Olton; Pat served as pastor in Takoka, Lawn, Baird, and in Olton. He also had a radio program out of Merkel. Pat and Julia had four children: Ezequiel, Ruth, Grace, and Pat, Jr. Their first child died very young and she is buried in Olton, Texas.

Margaret, our oldest sister, met Milton Martinez in Dallas where she was working and staying with the Chapas. She and Milton were married in Olton (1954) and Bro. Godsey performed the wedding. Milton and Mague served in churches in Petty, Merkel, Stamford, Mineral Wells, and Victoria. Milton died at a young age (41) in Victoria of pneumonia. Milton and Mague had two boys: Reynaldo and Benjamin.

Richard, our oldest brother married Lovelia Zavaleta in 1954. Lovelia was Catholic so they were married by a priest in Littlefield, Texas, about 25 miles from Olton. At the time Rico was working at a local grocery store. In fact, the rest of his life he spent working at different grocery stores. Rico and Morena had four children: Ricky, Alicia, Laura, and Joe.

Martha met Carlos Gutierrez and they were married in Olton in 1964 by Bro. Godsey. Carlos was in the U.S. Army so they lived in German, Alaska, Killen, El Paso, and other parts. In fact, Angie was born in Germany and Cynthia was born in Hawaii; Victor was born in the states.

Luisa met Pete Anzaldua (from Cuero) and they were married by Bro. Godsey in 1964. Pete and Luisa had three children: Annette, Pete, Jr., and Jason.

Irene met Mario Garcia in Olton and Irene, thirteen, was too young to marry, but finally Dad and Mom gave their permission. They were married in Olton in 1964 by Bro. Godsey. Mario and Irene have two children: Victoria and Mario, II. Their first born, Susie, died as a 3-year-old.

Ever since I can remember, our parents would counsel and talk to us about marriage. I remember them saying, "We don't care who you marry, as long as that person is a believer in Jesus Christ." I always remembered the advice of my parents regarding marriage. I had several girlfriends, and most were not believers, so marriage never entered my mind. One year Larry Perez, a close friend of mine, and I drove from Olton, Texas to Bronte, which was near San Angelo, to see our girlfriends, Hortensia and Rebecca Dominguez. That night Larry and Becky decided to elope. They strongly encouraged me and Hortensia to join them. They kept saying, "Come on, Joe, we can make it." It was a lot of pressure on me, but I said no since Hortensia was not a believer.

Bro. Glen and Oralia were always close to our family in helping us with all kinds of family problems. As we all know, when family members begin to leave the nest, all kinds of problems develop. Of course, it is always a good time because grandchildren begin to arrive. The first grandchildren for Richard and Maria Alcorta were Ezequiel Gloria and Ricky Alcorta.

For the last six years or so (2004-2010) Liandra and I frequently visited Bro. Glen and Oralia in their home in Plainview. Both were in declining health. Bro. Godsey had diabetes, and Mary had cancer. Liandra would always take flowers for Mrs. Godsey. Liandra's philosophy has always been: "Let's take them flowers while they can see them and smell them. When they die, it is too late."

Oralia Godsey passed away on October 22, 2010; and Bro. Godsey passed away about a month later on November 20, 2010. I was privileged to have participated in their respective funerals. Lynn Gayle, their son, surprised me and gave me Bro. Godsey's gold pocket watch. I will cherish it very much. Bro. Godsey also had instructed his family that *I* receive all of his memoirs.

In my book, *Words of Wisdom from a Cool College Professor* I wrote the following about Brother Godsey:

I met Rev. Glen E. Godsey in Olton, Texas, in 1952. At that time, Rev. Godsey served as the pastor of a small Mexican Baptist mission in Olton. Our family worshipped in that mission. I learned many things from this minister and his wife Oralia. They truly loved people. Brother Godsey helped the Hispanics as well as the Anglos.

Something happened in the fall of 1954 that I will never forget. Some local citizens invited Brother Godsey to come to downtown Olton. In front of the town square, the people gave Brother Godsey a brand new 1954 Chevrolet. I could not believe it! At that time I did not understand why they had done this. Now I do!

Brother Godsey worked as a pastor, an evangelist, a singer, a counselor, a comedian, and a great cook! Rev. Godsey grew up in Bristol, Tennessee. The military drafted him, and he went to serve our country. He told me that he never wore shoes until he joined the Army! He was wounded in the war and sent to a hospital in New Mexico. At the hospital he met his future wife, Maria Oralia Felix.

After marriage, Bro. Godsey felt the call to minister to the Mexican American people. He did not know how to speak the Spanish language, so he enrolled at Wayland Baptist College, located in Plainview, Texas. While a student at college, he preached at our church in Olton. We grew up with his three children: David, Yolanda, and Lynn Gayle. Later, the Godseys adopted Corina and Betty. His oldest son, David, died in an automobile accident, and Lynn Gayle serves as a pastor of a Hispanic church in Ennis, Texas.

I learned a lot from this man. Besides my parents, he has had a big influence in my life. He has taught me a lot about work, morals, character and integrity. I left Olton to attend college, but we have kept in touch over the years.

Rev. Godsey and his wife reside in Plainview, Texas. Both now in their 80's, remain strong. Rev. Godsey works as Associate Director of Missions for The Caprock-Plains Baptist Area. Both are in declining health, but their spirits remain high. My wife and I try to visit them two or three times a year, and we always receive a great blessing when we fellowship with them. They are really special. We laugh so much when we are together!

On Nov. 3, 2001, my wife and I attended the special reading of a Plainview city proclamation by Mayor Lloyd Woods changing the name of

San Felipe and Escuela Streets to Avenida Godsey and unveiling of street signs. Yes, sir! They named a street after this preacher!

Godsey's daughter, Yolanda, in an essay wrote about her father, which appeared in the 1998 June *Plainview Daily Herald,* said, "This gentleman has a big gentle heart made of gold. He rarely takes offense and forgives easily. One could spit in his face and the following moment he would speak to you as if nothing had happened. Some might think him a wimp, yet he possesses might and power for his strength comes from within. He says, "God fights my battles." She continued to say, " . . . This big, lovable, red-faced, jolly man has a beautiful attitude and outlook on life. He believes "If you can't say something good about someone then don't say anything at all."

Dealing with unkind remarks or rudeness or in suggesting how we might handle the same, Glen Godsey says, "I wouldn't lose sleep over it!" He lives by what he preaches and his lifestyle teaches the most effective sermon."

Brother Godsey is truly a great role model. He has done so much for society.

University Baptist Church, Abilene, Texas

When I came to college at Hardin-Simmons, I had received a Latin American scholarship, and one requirement was that I had to attend an Anglo Baptist church for one year. I joined University Baptist Church which was very close to Hardin Simmons. We had a great preacher, and I attended the Sunday school class for university students, but I don't remember who was the Sunday school teacher.

Of course, it was when I was attending University Baptist that I saw Liandra for the very first time. One Sunday as I was leaving church, I saw her and other nurses walking toward their nurses dorm. So, big thanks go to the WMU and University Baptist for introducing Liandra and I. I always say that God has a sense of humor.

Ambler Baptist Church, Abilene, Texas

During the year, at night I started attending Ambler Baptist Mission, which was a few blocks away from University Baptist. It was a mission of First Baptist Church and the Rev. Bill Ybarra was the pastor. Soon I became active with the mission and the youth work. They made me the youth director. We had get-together on Fridays for Bible study, refreshments, and different activities.

When Liandra and I were engaged to get married, the mission, under the leadership of Mrs. Bill (Sarah) Ybarra, gave us a big wedding shower. We were really excited and surprised. We became real close friends with the Ybarras and their three children: Debbie, Dianne, and David. Even after they left Ambler we kept in touch with them.

Bro. Ybarra died on August, 2009. I felt very bad that I could not attend his funeral in Ft. Worth. Liandra and I were out of town in New York visiting another one of our former ministers.

We had great times at Ambler in meeting wonderful people. I remember that on Sunday nights different church members would invite the Hardin-Simmons University students to go and eat at their house after the night service. Those were great times. In most cases Liandra and I were invited to most houses and we had a great time. I remember Elias Cancino; he was a great young man who always made us laugh with his jokes. He also used to work at a flower shop and many times on Saturday nights he would bring a truck full of flowers for us to keep or to give away. These flowers were damaged or out of date so they were to be thrown away. Elias would bring them to our house!

Families who I remember from Ambler Baptist were: Frank and Ruth Castillo; Eusebio and Carmen Miramontez; Gene and Concha Sanchez; Daniel and Josefina Ramirez; Jesse and Benita Molina, Wally and Ann Espinoza; Eliseo and Audelia Martinez; Moises and Hipolita Perez; Roberto y

Thelma Torres; Gilberto y Aurora Torres; Richard and Irma Cordero; Henry and Alicia Davila; Rudy and Betty Morado; Julian and Charlotte Bridges; Felipe and Nellie Zendejas; Rogelio and Consuelo Castillo; Mrs. Esther Gonzales; Epigmenia Martinez; Miss Petra Martinez; Miss Leonor Martinez; and Margarita Martinez. Of course most of these families had children who are now adults and have their own families.

We really enjoyed our church worship at Ambler. We saw it grow and develop into a strong church. There was closeness among the members. Many times on Sunday afternoon several of us "young ones" would go to the park at Sears across the church or to Hardin-Simmons and play touch football. If the Dallas Cowboys were playing, we would schedule our playing time around the game.

One year I decided to organize a men's softball team at Ambler. Our first coach was Cecilio Martinez. His son, David, was our best player. David played shortstop and many times would hit homeruns. Another year Eliseo Martinez, his brother was the coach. One year I was the coach. The older players were slow and we had to depend on the young ones to carry us through. I remember Elias Garrido, Pap Jones, Alex Vasquez, and Richard Cordero our best players. Gene and Jimmy Smith, brothers, and brothers-in-law of mine also were good players.

Well, one year, it paid off, and we won the championship. We were very excited because we beat one of Pioneer Drive Baptist teams. The softball league was formed by some local churches and the YMCA did the schedule and the tournaments. It was a good activity. I believe each church paid a fee of $60 to participate. The men's softball team helped the church to grow and to develop in a positive way. There was a good atmosphere at the games. Family members enjoyed seeing their loved ones playing the game.

For many years Liandra and I were elected to serve as counselors of the youth. So, we would take the young people to the youth camps and to Congreso. For camp we would normally go to Mt. Lebanon, outside of Dallas. Beside the Bible studies, and worship services, we participated in different competitions in volleyball and basketball. One year, our basketball team (three in a team) won the championship. (Freddy Stokes, nephew of Liandra was one of the players.) There was also competition in football but we did not have enough to field a team. Teams from San Antonio and San Angelo were always tough teams to beat.

At camp and at Congreso there was always a concert or a band playing on the last day of camp. At camp on Thursday nights it was pillow fights or water gun fights at the baseball field. It was through Youth Congress, camp, and Convencion that we got close to a lot of Hispanic Baptist State leaders.

At Ambler Baptist we always looked forward to our annual church revivals. Some of our outstanding evangelists were Rudy Sanchez, Rudy Hernandez, Roberto Garcia, Jose Rivas, Paulino Bernal, Pablo Cuevas, and Victor Rodriguez.

Another exciting thing that happened at Ambler was the forming of a youth music group whose name was Alpha and Omega. It was made up by Becky Bridges, Debbie Bridges, Elias Cancino, and Josh Martinez. And . . . . They were good! They were asked to play at the annual Youth Congress meeting and at other youth activities.

Cecilia Yvette Alcorta
Celebrates Quinceañera

At Ambler Baptist in 1980, our daughter Cecilia celebrated her 15th birthday with a Quinceañera. It was a very special time. She had fourteen couples her age who accompanied her, and she and her escort were the fifteenth couple. I said a few words in the church and then Bro. Paul Vasquez presented a family sermon. We had a delicious dinner afterwards for everybody. In the Hispanic culture, turning fifteenth for a girl is an exciting day. Most families celebrate in many different ways. Depending on the family, it can be a simple happy birthday with a cake and cookies or it can be a big deal at church with music, mariachis, orchestra, and a dance. Following is the printed invitation:

Mr. and Mrs. Joe H. Alcorta
Request the Honor of Your presence at a
Special Religious Service of Thanksgiving
To the Lord for the Fifteenth Anniversary
Of the Birth of their Daughter
Cecilia Yvette
The Service will be on
Saturday, September 13, 1980 at 11:00 a.m.
Ambler Baptist Church
2150 Park Street
Abilene, Texas

In our case, we wanted to express our gratitude to God for our daughter Cecilia. We also wanted to place her in His hands. Following is part of the story that appeared in *The Family Newsletter*, dated September, 1980.

LETTER FROM LONNIE REGARDING CECILIA'S QUINCEAÑERA

(Liandra Alcorta, mother of Cecilia wrote in Spanish and in English a letter of thanks to family members who made the Quinceañera a success)

Muy amados hermanos,

Les doy mis profundas y muy sinceras gracias por su apoyo y ayuda en la Quinceañera de Cecilia. Fue una ocasión muy gozosa y hermosa para nosotros.

Quizás algunos de ustedes no comprenden porque le dimos una Quinceañera a Cecilia. Les quiero decir que la idea comenzó conmigo. Quería darle a demostrar a Cecilia que los Creyentes también pueden divertirse en tal manera que Dios sea glorificado. Además fue un tiempo para dar gracias a Dios por los años que nos ha prestado a Cecilia y al mismo tiempo que ella tomara la oportunidad de re dedicar su vida al Señor. La comida y la fiesta que siguió fue para celebrar su cumpleaños.

Los que no pudieron estar con nosotros se perdieron de un hermoso servicio y una buena comida. Les extrañamos mucho pero al mismo tiempo comprendemos que muchos tenían que trabajar. Cecilia parecía una princesa. Se miraba muy hermosa. Le quiero dar las gracias especialmente a los siguientes:

Sammy y Anita. The ring you chose was beautiful. It was so dainty, just ideal for C.Y. Thank you for having a part in her Quinceañera.

Rico y Morena. The watch was exactly what she was hoping for with some added features that really made her happy. Thanks so very much.

Jimmy y Sarah. Thank you for paying for the shoes she had chosen. I know you could have gotten them cheaper at Sears, but I appreciate your thoughtfulness. And Sarah, thanks a million for helping me make all those thousands of enchiladas. Well . . . maybe not quite a thousand but a whole lot anyway. I appreciate it very much Sarah!!! Also for helping serve. Thanks again.

Martha. The satin pillow is beautiful and something she can keep for a long time. Thanks also for letting Angie be in her court of honor. It meant a lot to Cecilia because as you know she and Angie have always been real close. Thanks for helping in the serving and cleaning. I appreciate it greatly.

Pete and Luisa. A big thanks to you (and to Pete for allowing you to come) for making the sacrifice of a long trip so that Annette could participate. Thank you for serving and helping. I appreciate it so very much. Your being here also gave us the opportunity to visit.

Bernabe and Mague. Thanks for coming and for bringing Ben and "Fish" with you. It gave us the opportunity to see you and them and to see their two precious children. I can't believe those "fuzzes" are so cute.

Last but not least, **Mom and Dad**. Gracias por la Biblia que le presentaron a Cecilia. También por sus oraciones y el ánimo que nos dieron. También a **Gene and Rachel** for having part in getting the Bible. Special thanks to **Rachel** for helping serve. I appreciate your hard work very much. If you decide to give Jeanette a Quinceañera, I'll be more than willing to help.

Que Dios los bendiga ricamente. Les agradezco muchisimo.

Sinceramente,

Lonnie

Editor's note: Mike Olivares, Benita Stokes, and Luisa Burns, brother and sisters of Lonnie, also helped a lot with the Quinceañera. Mike Olivares III (nephew) also helped with the cleaning up.

Program of Cecilia's Quinceañera

Preludio ——————————Carlota Bridges y Martín Cuéllar

Bienvenida ——————————Rdo. Pablo Vásquez

Himno Especial ——————————Elías Cancino y Martín Cuéllar

Lectura Bíblica ——————————Cecilia y el Rdo. Vásquez

Himno Congregacional ————Elias Cancino

Oración de Consagración ———Dr. Julian Bridges

Palabras Paternales——————Joe H. Alcorta

Canto Especial ——————————Elías Cancino y Martín Cuéllar

Sermón ——————————Rdo. Pablo Vásquez

Bendición ——————————Rdo. Bill Ybarra

Postulado ——————————Carlota Bridges

50th Wedding Anniversary Celebration of Mr. and Mrs. Richard Alcorta

Also at Ambler Baptist Church, on November 1981, our parents Richard and Maria Alcorta celebrated their 50th Wedding Anniversary. Rev. Glen Godsey, a former pastor did the ceremony. Charlotte Bridges, a close friend of the family helped with the wedding plans. (The following is some short excerpts from *The Family Newsletter, Vol. VIII, dated November, 1981*):

"Some words of praise that were heard after the celebration were: pretty, nice, very nice, bonita, tremenda, beautiful, perfect, exciting, touching, unforgettable, emotional, and well organized." And it was a beautiful occasion, and all that because many people put a lot of work into it; there was a great amount of cooperation—with ideas, suggestions, time, and money. The idea of the celebration started two or three years ago when it was suggested that such event could take place. A date and place were selected, and the wedding invitations were printed. Mickey Martinez from Dallas printed the beautiful invitations. Maria began to dream the wedding.

. . . The wedding rehearsal on Friday night was a lot of fun. Charlotte Bridges, former member of Ambler and a friend of the Alcortas for the last ten years, was in charge of directing the wedding celebration, and she did an outstanding job, plus her friendly smile kept everyone "loose and cool." Cookies and coffee were served after the rehearsal; and then the tables and chairs at the church were set up for the dinner for the following day. Earlier in the day, several people had helped in moving church furniture around to make room for the wedding meal and reception.

Saturday was the exciting day! As usual everyone was in a rush getting ready. Luisa and Rachel visited the beauty shop. Pat Jr. wanted a haircut.

Zeke needed some new boots. Luisa needed to pick up her dress. Mague didn't like the way the dress looked. Anyway, everyone looked beautiful for the occasion. Maria Alcorta woke real early and at 7:30 she was at the church cooking the rice because she wanted it to be just right. All by herself a few weeks before, she had made over 40 dozen tamales. A few days before she had instructed Sarah to buy "white potatoes ("they are the best kind") for the salad to be used at the family dinner. Lala (Morena's mother) was also early at the church helping cooking the "frijoles."

At the church, Sarah, Rachel and Martha dressed the bride. Maria got a little perturbed because she had forgotten her special kind of perfume she intended to wear for the occasion. Fortunately a substitute was found. Very touching and emotional was the scene in the dressing room when Ester Sandoval (Maria's sister) went in to see Maria dressing. It was a beautiful sight . . . and a few tears were exchanged.

Meanwhile in the auditorium, fighting as to who would sit the prettiest girls, were ushers Joe Angel Alcorta, Joe Alcorta, Jr., and Pete Anzaldua, Jr. They were specifically given instructions (in writing) by the bride as to where to sit some family relatives and guests.

Cecilia Yvette and Angie, as receptionists, had a good time receiving the guests and the gifts and looking at the good looking guys.

Some tension and apprehension was felt right at 11:00 a.m. before the wedding because Mague and Julia had not arrived. Playing prelude music were Martin Cuellar, H-SU student from Del Rio, was at the piano; and Petra Martinez, church member and organist from Abilene was at the new organ which was purchased by Ambler the day before.

The bride gave the go-ahead for the wedding to begin at 11:15. Mague came in a few minutes before and the wedding procession started. A few minutes earlier, Zeke Gloria had taken off in search for his Mom. Outside of Merkel he spots her car, crosses the highway median to overtake her (a trucker on a CB jokes with him), and he races at all kinds of speed toward Ambler. The ride reminded one of a James Bond movie car chase. Julia runs in to the church; Charlotte quickly helps her to dress, and before one can say jackrabbit, Julia is dressed and she sneaks in her place at the altar as Maria is reciting the words from a hymn.

As the ceremony began, Rev. Glenn Godsey, Ricardo Alcorta Sr. (groom), and best man Ricardo Alcorta Jr. march in from the front, and all three men faced the congregation and are anxiously waiting for the bride.

First to march in is Lovelia Alcorta, matron of honor. Then, from the oldest to the youngest sons and daughters and their spouses (or escorts) march in . . . . Jimmy Ray Smith, the ring man, follows with Jeanette Smith alongside who marches on to the piano. Dropping little flowers petals in front of the bride were flower girls Vickie Garcia and Cynthia Gutierrez. (Someone had forgotten the flower baskets!!! Mario and Pete race off to the flower shop to buy them . . . $18.00 worth!!! Jimmy and Joe "stole" some roses from Ambler and rapidly devoured them for the pedals).

As Maria, the bride, gets ready to enter, Jeanette Smith is now at the piano playing the wedding march. (Later she said she was scared to death but that she had prayed all the time that she would not make a mistake . . . of course that morning she had practiced about 100 times) All the daughters and sons and spouses were up front facing the bride . . . this was a very emotional time for most family members as the bride slowly walked down the aisle. As one person described her: "She looked like a doll." Rosa Gonzalez, the bride's sister, was thinking: "If she is so beautiful now, I wonder how she must have been 50 years ago?" The bride's dress was off white with long lace sleeves, and her neckline and waistline were trimmed in gold color. Her veil was a matching off white. For something borrowed she wore Sarah's diamond earrings. The white Bible she was carrying was the same one Rachel carried in her wedding. Something new was the dress and a gold necklace given to her by Luisa. And all under the innocent face and veil she was wearing the traditional garter, a courtesy of the Rios Dress Shop.

Needless to say, the ladies looked just beautiful in their long pink dresses, and the men were just as handsome in their black tuxedoes and pink shirts. All the little ones were just dressed so cute. Morena's dress was a long lacy beige dress because she was the maid of honor. Mague's dress was a beautiful light maroon. Everyone probably thought Mague's dress was different because she was the oldest, but in reality, she just didn't like the way the pink dress fit.

. . . . Reynaldo Martinez with guitar in hands then sang a special song in Spanish for his grandparents. It was touching . . . caused more tears! Josh later was to say that he was more nervous at this wedding than he was at his own. After this special song, Joe H. Alcorta ("el doctorcito") surprised the bride, groom and attendants as he read for the first time a poem he had written for this special occasion, and it was dedicated to his parents. In brief, the poem tells the history of Ricardo, Maria and family, and it praises their good and successful life.

. . . . After the famous kiss, and the conclusion of the ceremony, Rev. Godsey prayed, and Annette Anzaldua concluded the prayer by singing the

Lord's Prayer in Spanish . . . . After the ceremony, Bernabe asks the groom, "Are you ready for the honeymoon?" Ricardo quickly answered: "What honeymoon? I am ready to go home and get some rest!"

Pictures were taken in the auditorium after the wedding, and the guests either watched or were in line for the wedding dinner. Busy in the serving line and kitchen were Carmen Miramontez, Benita Molina, Aurora Torres, Thelma Torres, Consuelo Castillo, and Virginia Hatchett all members of Ambler.

Later in the afternoon, around 5:00 o'clock most family members were at Rose Park recreation center getting ready for the evening meal. The big honcho cooking the meat was Rico.

. . . . Ricardo and Maria would like to express their appreciation to everyone that attended the celebration, and to thank everyone that had a small or a large part in it. They said words cannot express all the good feeling they felt toward everyone.

Rev. Bill Ybarra Resigns as Pastor at Ambler Baptist Church

As in most small churches, there seems to be some kind of conflict that starts among the congregation and it always involves the pastor. And that is what happened with Bro. Bill Ybarra at Ambler. Bro. Bill's brother-in-law accused him of some stuff. It was found out that Bro. Bill had not been given his tithe; and that he had been working too much as a painter without the church's permission. At least twice a member from First Baptist Church had helped Bro. Bill to get out of debt. Bro. Ybarra had no choice but to resign. In defense of Bro. Ybarra, I might say that First Baptist Church never paid him enough to support his family.

Rev. Ruben Hernandez,
New Pastor at Ambler Baptist

The next pastor of Ambler Baptist Church was Rev. Ruben Hernandez. He came from the Houston area. He was well educated and very well organized. His English and Spanish were excellent! At one time he had studied to be a medical doctor. Under his ministry the mission became a church and four deacons were elected. My dad, Richard Alcorta, Felipe Zendejas, Moises Perez, Gene Smith (my brother-in-law) and I became the first deacons of the church. We went through some intensive training. We had to read the well know book on deacons by Naylor, and then we had our ordination service.

My pastor, the Rev. Ruben Hernandez wrote the following on a Bible he gave me on the occasion of my ordination as a deacon: "Esta Biblia es presentada en la fecha de su ordenación como diacono. Rogamos a Dios que por su conducta personal y por el desempeño de su oficio como diacono pueda hacer que siempre podamos llamarle "nuestro diacono" con orgullo.

Misión Bautista Ambler
Abilene, Texas
10 de noviembre de 1974

The church grew under the ministry of Rev. Hernandez. Several church members travelled with First Baptist Church choir to Latin America. The music program also grew. An outstanding choir was formed.

Something again happened with Rev. Hernandez. It was known that he had strong feelings toward a secretary that worked with him at the church. Soon there was division between the four deacons and the congregation. Bro. Hernandez did not have a choice but to resign.

The Rev. Paul Vasquez,
new pastor at Ambler Baptist

The next pastor of Ambler Baptist was Rev. Paul Vasquez, a graduate of Hardin-Simmons. I was a member of the pulpit committee who drove to Mineral Wells to hear him preach. We became close friends of the Vasquez. In fact, my wife and Mrs. Vasquez continue to be best friends.

After several years at Ambler, Bro. Vasquez felt a calling to become a hospital chaplain. He asked the church for some time off to study, and to participate in the chaplain program. Most church members were against Bro. Vasquez taking time off from the church. Bro. Vasquez resigned and entered the chaplain school at Hendrick Medical Center.

It was also about this time that other problems surfaced at the church and Liandra and I decided to leave the church. There were some things done and accepted in the church business meeting that Liandra and I did not agree. The church elected a couple to be youth counselors and the husband was not a believer. My wife and I totally disagreed with that. It was very hard to leave because we had been members for about 20 years. I had been a Sunday school teacher and Training Union leader for many years. At that time I felt like my leadership was not accepted. We could sense an evil spirit in the congregation.

The next pastor to serve Ambler was Rev. Charles Maciel. He came from New Mexico. His son, Rene came to HSU to play basketball, and later stayed as the head of student recruitment.

Elmcrest Baptist Church, Abilene, Texas, 1981-91

After much prayer and discussion, my wife encouraged me to to step aside, and we visited Elmcrest Baptist Church. Rev. T.C. Melton, the pastor, visited us in our home after our first visit to the church and he told me, "Joe, church members are like preachers, sometimes God will tell you, I am finished with you here, and you need to move on. I need you in another place." His words helped us to join Elmcrest. The Lord led us there and we joined the church with gladness.

Liandra and I felt real weird worshiping with Anglo people. We were accustomed to worshipping with Hispanic people. We missed all the hymns that we sung in Spanish. Singing and praying in English was very difficult for us. We also felt that the Anglo people were not accepting us. But . . . little by little all that went away and we came to love the church and its people. We made many close friends.

It was at Elmcrest that we became very close friends of Felix and Linda Villalovos; and Bert and Georgia de la Vega. Of course, our pastor, Bro. Melton and his wife Mary Frances were very sweet people. Our assistant pastor, Burtis Williams and his wife Linda also were close friends. Bro. Burtis has helped our family many times. He is a great family counselor.

Very soon I was asked to teach an adult Sunday school class. I began to learn a lot under Bro. Burtis Williams and Brad Waggoner. It was in this church that I began to grow more. They challenged the members in different directions. I remember we attended a conference at the local civic center with Bill Gothard on the subject of Basic Youth Conflicts. It helped me a lot in my Christian walk. One thing I learned from Bill was that everything belonged to God.

After attending the conference, later in the week as I was jogging, I began to talk to God and I also began to give God everything that I possessed. I cannot explain it, but it seems like a big, big load fell off my shoulders and I kept running and running. The last thing I gave God was our family cat which I disliked very much. To make a long story short, I will tell you that soon that cat left our house in good hands! It seems like a very simple thing—everything belongs to God, so He will take care of it! That is easy to say, but it is very hard to do!

It was at Elmcrest Baptist that we got to hear great men like Jack Taylor, W. A. Criswell, Peter Lord, Manley Beasley, Angel Martinez, S. M. Lockridge, and others. The group Life Action Ministry led by Jim St.Clair also ministered in our church. The famous comedian Dennis Swanburg also entertained us a couple of times.

Brad Waggoner challenged me into Scripture memory. I remember attending a Sunday afternoon class with Brad. Within a year I was accepted as one of the church deacons. There were about 25 deacons in the church. Most of them were good men.

Joe, Adriel, and Andrew became very active with the youth. At times Adriel and Andrew sang specials in front of the church. The three boys participated in weekend retreats. Ray Johnson, the youth minister, was very close to our sons. I remember one day, Ray came over to our house to help put a basketball goal. Years later, Ray came back to Elmcrest as their pastor.

It was one summer that Joe attended a Super Summer camp with his cousin Marla Burns from the Austin area. Joe returned a changed person. He came and got rid of all of his secular music. It was Joe and Adriel who encouraged us to listen to Christian music. Since Adriel lives with us, he keeps up with the latest in Christian music. I personally listen to American Family Radio (91.3), and to KGNC (88.1). In our bedroom television we often are tuned in to Trinity Broadcasting Network.

Rev. Dale Suel, pastor at Elmcrest Baptist

After thirty-five years at Elmcrest, Bro. Melton thought it was time for him to step down and invite a younger man with more energy and new ideas for the church. Bro. Melton resigned in 1986. I was elected to serve as one of the 11 members on the church pulpit committee. After many applications and a lot of prayer we drove to Oklahoma City to hear Rev. Dale Suel preach.

Bro. Suel came to our church and preached one Sunday morning. We called him and the church voted with a big majority for him to be our pastor. A week before moving to Abilene Kathy lost her dad, and her mother "Granny" came to live with them. Bro. Suel and his wife Kathy had two boys, Chris and Tim—they both were teenagers.

We really enjoyed Bro. Suel's preaching and leadership. Everything seems to be going well until we had a deacons meeting without Bro. Suel present. I learned that some of the deacons were unhappy with Bro. Suel and wanted him to resign. I quickly asked questions like, "Has he been unfaithful to his wife? Has he stolen some money? Has he been drinking? Or has he committed a grave sin?" The answers to my questions were, "No." Then I said, "Well, what is the problem?"

I never got a good answer. But as in most churches, there normally is a click that runs the church. If things are not done the way they want to, or like things have been done for a long time, they get very unhappy. That is what happened at Elmcrest. The "Powers to be" did not like or accept brother Suel or his family. Bro. Suel could not please them. Two things happened that were used to add fuel to the fire. One was that the music was different and by mistake college students had served unleavened bread for the Lord's Supper.

To make things a little worse, and unknown to a lot of us, was that the Suels were having a lot of problems with their son Tim. Tim had gone with the wrong crowd and was into drugs. I felt so bad when I found this out. I don't know if the church members helped or contributed to the problem. With the Lord's help Tim finally overcame the habit and became a strong Christian leader. He helped in leading the music and some members did not like the modern chorus type.

The deacons meetings were turning out to be heavy discussions between them and Bro. Suel. I began to feel very unconfortable as we attended meetings. There were four of us, Earl Garrett, Rodney Cosper, Jack Goodridge, and myself who tried to stand up for Bro. Suel but it was to no avail.

Upon someone's advice, a mediator from the outside was called in to try to help with the situation. That did not help much, because the opposition had already talked to the mediator and had basically agreed to bring up the matter before the church for a vote. On a Sunday night, the opposition brought all the trouble makers and a lot of members who had not come to church in a long time and the pastor was voted out. It was sad . . . very sad. I felt terrible. It was a very low point in my life. I didn't know what to do. Under that situation, we did not last long—clearly the devil was in the middle of this. I wrote a letter which read about the injustices the deacons had done to Bro. Suel. I explained why our family could no longer stay and support the church. Bro. Suel and family started attending Beltway Park Baptist Church and we followed. Liandra and I joined Beltway Park on November 30, 1997.

Soon the Suel family moved to College Station where Chris, their oldest son, was attending school. Bro. Suel obtained a full time job in the education department of Texas A&M, and Kathy became an elementary school teacher. Later Bro. Suel became the pastor of Steeple Hollow Baptist Church in Bryan. It was an older congregation, and there were very few children or young people in the church. The people accepted the Suels, and in fact, the congregation built a new parsonage for the Suels. Church members had a hard time accepting change and growth.

In 2009, Bro. Suel accepted to be the pastor of Baptist church in Buffalo, New York. In August of 2009, Liandra and I flew to Buffalo to visit the Suels. The Suels treated us like royalty. We stayed in their home. They gave us a great tour of Buffalo and also took us to Niagara Falls! Now, that was a treat! We enjoyed worshipping with them on that Sunday.

Beltway Park Baptist Church

When we joined Beltway, it was very small and declining. The church also had gone through a very rough time, and they were heavy into debt. They did not have many teachers. Right away I was given a Sunday school class of adults. Since then I have been teaching an adult Sunday school class at the church. We have had as few as eight and sometimes we have over twenty.

On Wednesdays nights, I teach a group of men. We have been together for about eight years. Some men come and go, but some stay. Here are the regulars right now: Jim Steadman, Bob Clark, John Ward, Max Deanda, Don Helow, and myself. Every once in a while we will have a visitor or two. We have studied many books. Originally, an elder, Ray Templeton started the men's class and then he passed it on to me. These are some of the books we have studied: *A Man's Guide to the Spiritual Disciplines* by Patrick Morley; *Walking Wisely* by Charles F. Stanley, *His Needs Her Needs* by Willard F. Harley; *Uncommon* by Tony Dungy; *Man to Man* by Charles R. Swindoll; and *100 Bible Verses Everyone Should Know* by Heart by Robert J. Morgan.

Our original sanctuary at Beltway could hold around 200 people, but it seldom was full. When we joined we had a temporary pastor by the name of Steve Harding, a HSU graduate. He was a fire ball. We loved him very much. Before Steve Harding came, there was a lot of debt and the deacons had talked about shutting down the church. Much prayer was said and the church decided to continue.

In 1996 we called a young pastor by the name of Rev. David McQueen. Bro. McQueen was a graduate of Abilene Christian University. He had been serving as an assistant pastor in Lubbock in a non-denominational church. Little by little the church turned around and we started to grow. Soon we were having two services and then three to accommodate the people. It was not long until we built a larger auditorium, and again we had to have three services. So again in the year 2009 we added a large children's building plus adding more room to the auditorium, and adding a kitchen and a gymnasium. Now we are having two services; one at 9:00 a.m. and the second one at 11:00 a.m. with an average attendance of about 800 in each service.

One of my complaints at the church, and some other older members is that the music (drums and base) is too loud. We have complained and talked to elders but the answer is that they are ministering to the crowd that likes the loud music.

The administration of the church is now run by elders, and we also have several ministers: A minister for music, cell groups, university students, middle school and high school, and for children. The church is big and we do have many programs on a weekly basis. We have a weekly program for recovering addicts; divorce adjustment; a healing program; a men's breakfast; several women's studies. Of course, there are several programs for the youth. High School and college students have their own service on Wednesday night with plenty of loud music.

Even though we have Sunday school classes, the church pushes more cell groups. A cell group consists of 10 people or more. These groups are free to meet any time during the week. There are probably about fifty cell groups. Most do meet on Sunday nights. Liandra and I were very active with Earl and Charlene Garrett groups for a couple of years, and then we quit going. We have not gone for about two years.

Our church also sponsors several trips to the Holy Land, Australia, Mexico, and other parts of the world. We help support an orphanage in Reynosa, Mexico. Every year we give 100's of bags with goodies to the prisoners at French Robinson Prison.

At Beltway, two of our children and their families have joined. Joe and Amber Alcorta and their two girls are members. Roy and Cecilia Castillo and their three boys are members. Joe baptized Morgan and Jessica. I had the privilege of baptizing Michael. Joe, Morgan, and Jessica have attended summer youth camps, and other youth activities. Joe and Amber have also been cell group leaders. Their group met on Sunday afternoons.

The Woman of my Life
(8-10-10)

I tell my relatives and friends, "Don't come to my funeral." Then I explain. I want you to visit me when we can enjoy each other's company; when we can talk, and drink a cup of coffee. At funerals, most friends will say to relatives: "He/She was a good man/woman!" She/he did this or that—always good! The person in the casket can't hear these things!

For this reason I want to say some good things about my wife, Liandra.

I am a believer a person should encourage and say good things to a living person. And for that reason, I want to say some good things about the woman who has put up with me for 48 years. Liandra and I married on August 19, 1962 in First Christian Church in Breckenridge, Texas.

She graduated with excellent grades from Breckenridge High School. So, she is a loyal Buckaroo fan. She loves sports! She brags that in junior high and in high school, there were very few boys who could out run her!!!

With famous Coach Emery Ballard, Breckenridge High School added two more state football championships. My first teaching job was in Brownwood, Texas. One Friday night when the Lions were playing the Buckaroos, she asks me, "Which side are you sitting on?" I answered, "Honey, I am a teacher here in Brownwood, I need to sit on the Lions side." She said, "I am not going!"

Liandra is a hard working woman. Grass does not grow under her feet. As a teenager, every summer her family went to Ephraim, Wisconsin for the cherry harvest. Her Dad gave her and other family members a certain number of buckets of cherries to pick. She always completed her goal and then her sister, Benita was asking for help. Liandra often says, "Those were great days! It was like a vacation to me."

Liandra is a quilt maker. She has made quilts for our children and grandchildren. She has also quilted many more which she has given away. She also does cross stitching. She loves to cross stitch angels. Collecting angels of all types is also one of her hobbies.

Liandra is a registered nurse. One of her high school teachers got her a job as a nurse's aide in the Breckenridge hospital. Two or three teachers and church members helped Liandra with a scholarship so she could attend Hendrick School of Nursing in Abilene, Texas. Liandra loves the nursing profession.

For more than twenty years she was the assistant nurse for Dr. John O'Loughlin, a neurologist, and his associates Drs. Walter Loyola, Ruben Brochnor, Richard Pratt, and Quirico Torres. Most surgeries would last from one to three hours. But once in a while a procedure might last more than 8 hours without a bathroom break! She loved this type of surgery. The only thing she did not like was her beeper!

On many occasions, family members or close friends would request that Liandra be in the operating room with them as their surgery took place. Doctors knew Liandra so they gave her permission to be in the room. Patients felt more at ease, knowing that Liandra was present.

When our first child was born at Hendrick Medical Center, the director of the hospital went up to Liandra's room and gave her several boxes of diapers for the new girl. Now, that was exciting! Later in years, when one of our boys had diabetes, the operating crew from Hendrick collected money and purchased for us a glucometer. In those days the glucometers were very expensive.

After a brief retirement, Mr. David Adams, principal at Ortiz Elementary asked Liandra to become his school nurse. For more than 15 years she has been having fun taking care of elementary school children. The children love her! Liandra's biggest challenge is locating parents or grandparents when the children become sick. She has found out that many children are being reared by their grandparents.

During our early marriage years, we went car shopping. As my Dad had done before I was looking at several used cars. She said to me: "Joe, what are we doing in these used car lots?" I answered, "We are going to buy a used car!" She said, "No, we are not. We are going to buy a new car!" We brought a brand new 1964 Chevy Impala! I asked her, "You think we can make the $65 monthly payment?" She answered, "Sure, we can!"

She is a terrific cook! You name it, she can cook it or bake it. Enchiladas, tacos, lasagna, carne guisada, brisquet, fried chicken, flour tortillas, rice, roast and potatoes. She also has a great tamales and pancake recipe. On Sundays after church there is always a home cooked meal for family members and friends. The grandchildren love her home-made flour tortillas.

She is always looking out for me. She buys all of my clothes. Liandra taught me to give flowers to the living. While my Mother was alive, one day she told me, "Joe, we are going to give flowers to your Mother so she can enjoy them while she is living." Liandra still practices this custom with our close lady friends.

Liandra does not walk on water, but she is a great spiritual woman. She knows her Bible, attends church every Sunday, and she is a praying woman. She loves people, and she is always ready to give a helping hand. She loves to read, watch movies, and do yard work. She is the one that gathers and shells our pecans. She really enjoys riding the lawn mower, and I let her!

I am very blessed to have Liandra as my wife. How about you reader, what can you say good about your spouse?

My Daughter

I joke around that I will never forget my daughter's birthday because she has the same birthday as that former famous Dallas Cowboy coach, Mr. Tom Landry. And sadly enough all Americans now remember what happened on September 11, 2001.

As I am writing this book, I try to recollect the past 45 years of my daughter's life. I must admit that now I would do a lot of things different. It was while Cecilia was a little girl that I was working on my Master's and Ph.D.'s degrees. I was also serving as an Abilene City Councilman. That will tell you that I just did not spend enough time with her. And besides I was a rookie Dad; and as we all know, rookies make a lot of mistakes!

If I had to do it over again I would hug her a lot every day and I would talk to her and go out on dates with her. You see, that is what I have learned from reading many parental books; especially Dr. James Dobson latest book, *Bringing Up Girls*.

Though I would change some things, the memories I have with Cecilia are special. I remember my wife taking Cecilia on walks in the streets of Brownwood, Texas, while I studied Russian and English history in our small apartment. Our apartment was small and old! Well, our landlord accused Cecilia, while in her baby crib, of tearing paper from the wall!! Can you believe this? Not my daughter!

I remember teaching Cecilia to drive! The mistake I made was taking my wife with us. Cecilia did especially well that day until we were turning into our driveway. She missed the driveway and was driving directly into the house. That is when my wife got a "little excited" and started screaming from the back seat something like "Cecilia! Put on the brake!" Cecilia and I were laughing . . . I had confidence that Cecilia was going to apply the brake . . . and she did!

The next driving episode happened on a Sunday afternoon when I sent her to the grocery store for an item. A policeman called me and asked if I was the owner of a 1980 Park Avenue Buick. I assured him that I was. "Well," he said, "I have a young lady driving your car and she does not have a driving license, and your inspection sticker is out of date." I told the officer, "I will be right there." As I drove up, the officer asks me, "Is this your daughter?" I did not answer, and mysteriously I walk toward the car and peeked at Cecilia through the window. I turn to the officer and say, "Yes, sir, she is my daughter!" Our driving violation fine was a total of $7.50! Praise the Lord!

The day of her wedding, July 21, 1990, she and I were in the hall of Logsdon Chapel, Hardin-Simmons University. I kept telling myself, "I am not going to cry. I am not going to cry." Well, you guessed it, I did cry!

Today it is hard to believe and understand the following humorous story. Liandra and I were very strict with Cecilia. When she started dating, she always had to be in before midnight. At home she was not to receive any phone calls after 10:00 o'clock at night. Well, I caught her one day. I walked into her room one night after 10:00 and she had the phone under her covers talking!

One more surprise! When she was a freshman student at H-SU, I called her one Saturday night. I called her at 10:00, 11:00, and 12:00 o'clock, and there was no answer. I began to worry. Where is this girl? At 1:00 o'clock she answers the phone and I immediately began to question her. She answers very politely, "Dad, we do not have a curfew here!" Well, that was news to me! I learned something that night!

I am so proud of Cecilia. She has accomplished so much. She and Roy have raised three boys, and she has taught over twenty years. On December 18, 2010, she received her Master's degree in counseling from Sul Ross University. Before the graduation ceremony, I went back looking for her among the graduating students. I found her and we hugged. The first thing she told me was, "Dad, I am really sick!" And she was! But, there she was real cute with her cap and gown. She had driven all the way from Abilene to Alpine, Texas to march across the stage. She had also made arrangements so Liandra and I could eat with the family after the graduation.

I do not know how she does everything she does. She is a wife, a mother, and a teacher. For years she has been the taxi driver for her three boys as they played baseball, soccer, basketball, and football. Then she works hard at staying physically fit. She and Roy go to the gym to work out, and she tries to run every week. She and I have run several 5ks together. Up until two years ago, I could beat her, but now that has changed. She finishes about two minutes ahead of me!

But most of all, Cecilia and I are very close. There is not one week that goes by without us having a conversation on the phone. And up to now, she has never forgotten my birthday or Father's Day. She supports me in everything I do. I can count on her to be at the finish line during my marathons. One of the most pleasant memories was in Dallas when her son Roy (about 6 years of age) ran a few yards with me during my Dallas White Rock Marathon.

Cecilia always calls me to remind me about Liandra's birthday, anniversary, and Mother's Day. Of course she always asks, "Dad, what are you getting Mother for Christmas?" Cecilia is like her Mother in that she loves to give good gifts. She has given me some good ones! She has given me running shoes, running shorts, running socks, shirt and tie to match, and a barbecue pit.

Cecilia loves her brothers very much. Of course, she was the official baby sitter for Adriel and Andrew. When the boys were playing baseball, if she thought the coaches were not playing them their fair share, she would tell me, "Dad, you need to talk to the coach!"

For lent, one year she called me and asked, "Dad, what are you giving for lent?" I answered, "Can you do without sweets for several weeks." She answered, "Sure, why not!" So, we suffered together!

We as parents often wonder if we did a good job of raising our children. We are very happy when Roy's mother, Mrs. Emilia Castillo, brags to us about how Cecilia is so helpful and kind with her. At the recent death of Mr. Raul Castillo, Cecilia was right there with family members.

My Three Sons

I have always said that children are different from each other. I tell parents "Do not compare your children. Each one is different." I tell parents do not say to your son/daughter: "Why can't you be like your brother/sister?" It is not going to happen. God made us all different.

So with that brief introduction, allow me to tell you about my three sons. Joe is the oldest and Daniel Andres is the youngest. From first grade to the university, Joe was always an excellent student in school. When he was a junior at Abilene High School, I told him, "Joe, when are you going to find you a part time job?" You see his older sister had worked while she was a junior and senior in school.

He answered me, "Dad, I do not have time to work, I want to study hard and graduate at the top of my class." Joe graduated number 11 in a class of about 500. Liandra and I were blessed to have attended the Top Fifty Banquet which honored the top 50 graduating seniors in the Abilene area. Because he graduated in the top 10% of his class, Texas A&M awarded him a Presidential scholarship. Joe graduated from Texas A&M in 1991 with a major in Math. Joe and I nearly froze to death the first time we visited Texas A&M. We stayed overnight in a dormitory and we had no sheets or blankets, and there was no way to control the cold temperature!

Andrew and Adriel did graduate from Abilene High School but they were not racing to be at the top of the class. Andrew and Adriel attended Hardin-Simmons but did not graduate. Both acquired a few college hours, but college was not their thing.

Of the three boys, Andrew has had the most jobs. At an early age Andrew started out buffing tables at El Chico Restaurant in Abilene; then he worked for a short time for K-Mart. After high school he worked for Anderson Allied. For a couple of years he worked at Abilene Municipal Golf Course. He then went on a training program to become a restaurant manager for El Chico. He did that! He became kitchen manager and up front manager. His first job as a manager was in Oklahoma City. From Oklahoma he moved to Belton to work at the Killeen Logan Roadhouse; he also worked for Cheddar's but that did not worked out at all. He then got a job in Abilene installing security systems. Three years ago (2009) he went to Huntsville to work at another El Chico Restaurant. In November, 2010, he resigned at El Chico and came to Abilene and worked part time in construction with his friend Bryan whose company is Dally.

This year, 2011, on January 10 he started a job with Farmers Insurance. One thing I can say about Andrew, he is not afraid to start something different. He is a hardworking man!

I need to share this story about Andrew and his new boss, Chris. When in high school, Andrew came and asked if a friend could spend the night because his parents had kicked him out of the house. Andrew added, Dad, he is Black. I asked Andrew to bring his friend over and that we would talk. We did and I explained the house rules: No drinking, smoking, skipping curfew which was twelve midnight. That night I called Chris' dad and told him his son was with us and that he was safe. His Dad was very appreciative. Chris stayed with us for about a month. Later he graduated from Abilene High School and Abilene Christian University.

Chris now married, is a very successful business man with Farmers Insurance in Dallas, Texas. A few months ago Chris called Andrew and offered him a job. So, Chris is now serving as Andrew's boss and mentor! Recently I talked to Chris by telephone and expressed my appreciation for taking Andrew in.

Adriel began working at K-Mart, then at an auto shop selling parts. He has worked on and off at the gymnastic place teaching children gymnastics. It was at Wal Mart where he worked 8 years. In 2007, he asked Wal Mart to be put on sick leave time. Since that time, he has tried to get back with Wal Mart but they have not hired him back. He has worked a little at HSU bookstore, Target, and Allsup Store. Because of health problems (diabetes) in August, 2010, Adriel applied for disability with the local Social Security office. At the writing of this book, the application is still pending.

Though Joe did not want to work during high school, he did some yard work in the summers with the help of a 1966 Chevrolet pickup I bought for him from the maintenance department of H-SU for $300. Joe says the old clunker was a straight V-6, had no AC, needed to use the pliers to roll the window down; no radio, bald tires; the gas gage did not work; and it was baby blue in color. Later Mr. Raul Castillo painted the pickup A&M colors. While he was at Texas A&M he worked for the math department grading papers and tutoring students.

In Abilene he began his teaching career. In 1991 in the Spring he began by being a substitute teacher at Cooper High School teaching Algebra and Trigonometry; then in 1992 he was full time Mann Middle School teaching computer literacy and coaching. In 1999 he moved to Wylie High School as an assistant principal; and in 2000 he became principal at Wylie Intermediate School.

In 2004 Joe became the principal at Mann Middle School where he is today. Remember, this is where he attended middle school. This May, 2011, he will receive his doctoral degree in education from Tarleton College University in Stephenville, Texas. He now has begun to make applications to become a school superintendent.

All three sons married. Joe married Amber Burton on December 14, 1991. They have two daughters: Jessica and Morgan. Adriel married Lacy Marie Luck on July 5, 2001; they divorced in 2002; and they had one son, Ashby. Adriel also has another son, Caleb. Since March, 2002, Adriel and Ashby have lived with us. Andrew married Kayla McCoy on September 16, 2005. They have two children: Andrew and Rylie.

As I said at the beginning of this chapter, everyone is different. I will try to mention the differences that I have seen in them. Andrew grew with attention deficit disorder, so he could never be still for a minute. He grew up taking the medicine Ritalin. People with ADD are not organized, they lose stuff, and they have terrible handwriting. That was Andrew. So, at school he was not the greatest pupil. I knew all of Andrew's teachers real well. I got to see them often!

Adriel is left handed and they say that left-handed people are good with art and music, which describes Adriel. He has wonderful calligraphy and he can draw anything. He loves Christian music. He has a great collection of Christian artists, and has attended many Christian concerts. In church he used to sing specials. In Mann Middle School and in Abilene High he was in the band. One year at the annual Hispanic graduation dinner, Adriel played a special on the piano. He had not memorized that piece of music so he struggled . . . but he finished! His big brother Joe was at the piano turning pages for him.

All three boys participated in sports in school. Joe played football at Johnston Elementary. He also played football and basketball at Mann Middle School. He was the Quarterback of the 8th and 9th grade. I believe they won the city championship in football that year. His coach in basketball was Mr. Franklin. Later when Joe returned as principal, Mr. Franklin was still coaching. Mr. Franklin would tell me, "Mr. Alcorta, I could never teach Joe how to do a layup!"

Andrew loved basketball. We brought him an expensive North Carolina Hoosiers basketball jacket which he soon lost! He played at Franklin Middle School. I remember one time Mario Garcia and I went to see Andrew play. That day, Andrew was hot! He scored 39 points! That was a very exciting game to watch. I really never knew what exactly happened but Andrew and the high school coach never got along; so for that reason, Andrew made the team but the coach would not play him. I was so embarrassed on the first game of the season at Abilene High. I went and invited a bunch of people. Well, there was Andrew in his Eagle uniform, but the Coach did not play him one minute! If I was mad . . . I could imagine what was going through Andrew's head. Andrew eventually quit the team when the coach told him that he could stay with the team . . . but that he was not going to play!

When Andrew was 17 or 18 he helped me coach a basketball team (10-12 year-olds) at First Baptist Church, Abilene, Texas. It was his idea to have a team, but he could not coach because of his age. I was officially the coach but it was Andrew that coached the kids. We won the championship that winter. If I remember correctly, on the last game of the season, playing for the championship; because of foul trouble, we were one or two guys short on the court in the last two minutes. We still played and won!!!

While Andrew was good at basketball, Adriel excelled in gymnastics. At Abilene High School Adriel was in the gymnastics team. He participated in several competitions. He competed in the floor, horse, rings, and the parallel bars. He really enjoyed it until he had to quit because of an injury to his neck. He was doing the high bars, a fly away, sort like a flip and he landed on his head.

All three boys played Little League Baseball. Today, Andrew tells me that he hated to play . . . that he only played because I made him play . . . not true!! I always told my sons: "If you start something, or you sign up to play ball, then you need to finish the season." Andrew many times out in the field was looking at the birds or cutting flowers! Joe and Adriel were pretty good players. Joe normally played in the outfield; Adriel played first base or he was the pitcher. Joe played baseball all four years in High School. One year, Joe was not a starter and I asked him about it. He said: "Dad, wait till the six weeks grades come out and then I will be playing." He was right!

One year we were playing in the championship game and Adriel was pitching. We are ahead by one run. It was the last inning and our opponents were up to bat. There were two outs with the ninth batter up to bat and two men on base. Our coach instructed Adriel to walk the guy and the game would be over. Adriel threw way to the left. The opponents' fans started booing; and yelled, "Oh, come on, Coach, pitch to the guy, and give us a chance!" So our Coach told Adriel to throw strikes! Sure enough the guy hit the ball hard, but the short stop handled the ball and threw to second and the game is over. After the game, I told the coach, "Sir, I am very proud of you. You did the right thing."

Of course, sister Cecilia was always looking out for her brothers. If she felt the coaches were not playing her brothers enough time, she would tell me: "Dad, you got to speak up, you got to talk to the coach!"

Joe, Adriel, and Andrew enjoy playing golf. That is something we can do together. I have never been very good at it, but I like it. Joe is probably the better player and the most competitive. He did take a class in golf at Texas A&M. Since Andrew worked at a golf course, his golf game improved a lot! I believe only twice have we four been able to play together. Since Joe is the oldest, he and I have played the most golf. The most exciting golf course Joe and I have played in is The Garden of the Gods in Ruidoso, New Mexico. It is awesome!

Andrew surprised me three years ago when he and Kayla gave me a brand new set of expensive golf clubs. I was flabbergasted! I had never owned a new set of golf clubs! I had inherited Milton Martinez club when he died in 1972. Joe, in our earlier playing days, gave me a very nice driver. I won a brand new putter at a Credit Union convention, and Andrew recently gave me a "Ping" putter.

As we get older, we learn more about fatherhood. One day I was in Bryan, Texas, visiting with my former pastor, Bro. Dale Suel, and I told him: "You know, I really regret that while Joe was at Texas A&M I never attended a football game with him." Bro. Dale said: "What's wrong with going this year?" I really had never thought about it. Well, we did get tickets and Joe and I went to the Army-Aggie game in 2008. The following year we went again. This year, 2010, Joe and I had a lot of conflicts and we could not find a Saturday where we could attend a game. We will try again next year.

We have not been a fishing family but we have fished together. At different times in Twin Lakes, Colorado, Andrew, Adriel, Joe, and I went fishing for trout. I remember one year, Andrew caught a fish, and he would not let us kill it. Of course, as a Dad, I do remember spending a lot of time fixing the rod and reels and baiting the hooks. For Father's Day (twice) Joe asked his friend (and former teacher), Mr. Roy Franklin to take us fishing in Coleman Lake. On the way we stop to get a Hamburger. Mr. Franklin, an accomplished fisherman, took his boat and the equipment we needed. We sat out at the lake and Mr. Franklin told us what to do. We did it, and we caught a whole bunch of fish! In fact, around midnight, we had to start throwing back the ones we caught because of the fish limit. We had a great time!

I am not a big baseball fan but one year Joe took me to a Texas Rangers game in Arlington. At one time or another each son has run with me in a 5K race. I am very happy to report that every time I beat them!

Joe and Adriel went with me to Dallas to meet and interview Mr. Tom Landry, coach of The Dallas Cowboys. At that time I was writing the history of the Cowboys in Spanish. Joe and I went the first time. As we were entering the office building of The Cowboys, the Cheerleaders are returning from a performance. They are right there in front of us! The first thing I told Joe, "Where is the camera?" Joe answered, "Dad, I thought you had it!" Well, by the time Joe runs to the car to get the camera the girls are gone! Well, folks, that is just life!!!

Adriel, Liandra, Victor Gutierrez, and I went to see Coach Landry the second time. This time Victor had the camera and he took pictures of us with Coach Landry.

The saying, "Boys will be boys," is certainly true. And my three sons were not any different. Growing up, each one had his share of getting into some mischievous or some kind of trouble. For example . . . One son has a record for wrecking cars and getting speeding tickets.

One thing I appreciate of my three adult sons, we respect and love each other. As adults, now, we may have different ideas and opinions but we still talk and discuss openly in a civil manner.

Liandra's Family

It was in 1961 that I began to meet and know Liandra's family. I met Mr. and Mrs. Miguel Olivares on a weekend when I took Liandra from Abilene to Breckenridge to visit with her parents. Liandra was in nursing school. The first thing that impressed me was that on Sunday Mr. Olivares cooked a lot of meat on an outside home-made grill. As we sat to eat that

Sunday, he brought half of a barbecue chicken and placed it right on my plate. Remember, I grew up in a family of 10 children! So, we were lucky to get a chicken leg, much less half of a chicken! I said to myself, "Is this all mine?" He had also prepared some kind of steak and asked me if I wanted some. I politely said no.

Mrs. Olivares was very nice and quiet. That night I heard her tell Liandra, fix Joe's bed outside on the porch. Liandra answered, "Let Joe fix his own bad!" Mrs. Olivares got unto Liandra and told her, "No seas grosera! Ya te dije que fueras a hacerlo. Tú arreglala!" (Don't be impolite, I already told you to do it. You fix it)

Of course I met the whole Olivares family that Sunday afternoon, on August 19, 1962, when Liandra and I married. It was Jimmy and Mary who drove us around in Breckenridge, and helped us to hide our car at the Ridge Motel so no one would do anything to our car. After the wedding, they took us to the Ridge and there Liandra and I took off for the honeymoon.

I believe I met Jimmy Burns and his wife Mary (Liandra's sister) when we went to Ballinger and they took us to eat steak at Lowake. Jimmy had his Mother (Mrs. Gertrude Burns) here in Abilene so they came to visit her and us. Jimmy and Mary had two children: Marla and Jimmy Lee. Marla has never married. Jimmy Lee married and has one son. Marla graduated from San Angelo State University and the Baptist Theological Seminary from Ft. Worth, Texas.

For many years Jimmy was a butcher at Safeway and he worked in Ballinger and then drove to San Angelo where he worked for Safeway. After his death in 2002; Mary moved to Wimberly with her daughter Marla.

About thirty years ago (around 1980) the Olivares family started a Thanksgiving dinner which was held in Breckenridge the Sunday after Thanksgiving Day. The dinner was started a year or two before Mrs. Olivares passed away in 1977. Mr. Olivares passed away in 1986 and the dinners have continued. This was a good time to get to know everyone better. This is where I met Chacha (Alicia) and her family; and Alex Adamez and his family.

I did not know Jesse Olivares as well as the others. Jesse was the quiet one in the family. He married Alicia and they had a son, Jesse, Jr. Alicia was from Mexico and she could not speak English. "Little Jesse" married and had several children. Jesse died from a wrong medication in Dallas in 1999. Alicia died in 2005.

I got to know Benita, Liandra's youngest sister, in Abilene. Benita attended beauty school in Abilene; in Abilene she met Fred Stokes and they married. Fred and Benita adopted Gracie and they had Freddy. After marriage, Fred, Benita, Liandra and I vacationed together. We went to the Grand Canyon and Mexico City.

Both Freddy and Grace married. Freddy and his wife Yvette had five children: Myra, Freddy, Alexis, Nikoa, and Xavier. With her first marriage, Grace and Wilbert Lockridge had Dakota and Savanah. After a divorce Grace had Duran and Gabriel. Fred and Benita adopted Gabriel (Grace gave birth to Gabriel).

I met Richard and Charles Zapata, nephews of Liandra, in Breckenridge. Mr. and Mrs. Miguel Olivares had raised Richard and Charles after the death of their mother, Socorro (Liandra's youngest sister). Richard actually lived with us for several years in the 70's. He was going to Operating Room Technician school at Hendrick Medical Hospital. Richard served in the military (Navy) for several years. Richard married Nita and they have two adult children: Lauren and Jonathan.

I met Liandra's brothers, Mike, Jesse and their spouses, Sandy and Alicia at family gatherings. Mike and Sandy had one son, Kirk. From a previous marriage, Mike (and Gloria) had Mike and Lisa.

Lisa Olivares married Richard Sorrell and they had two daughters, Rachel, and Lindsey. Recently Richard and Lisa have divorced. Mike Olivares, II has been married twice. He has a daughter and a son. His son, Mike, III, married in 2005.

For many years Mike, Liandra's brother, was in the beer business. In Breckenridge he sold Jax Beer and in Mineral Wells he sold different kinds of beer and other soda pops. I got to know Mike and Sandy a lot better these last ten years. Often Liandra and I visited them in Mineral Wells, Texas. Mike got sick with cancer and went through rough times but with time he was healed. We would go and visit and we always prayed with him before leaving the house. In 2009 it was discovered that Sandy had Alzheimer disease. It was very sad to see her in this condition. Her illness progressed rapidly. She died in 2009. In the summer of 2010 Mike became friends with Gwen Rogers. She now lives with him and they have been good for each other.

Socorro Olivares Zapata, the oldest of the family died in 1945. She and her husband Johnny had two boys: Charles and Richard.

Changes that occur in our lives

There are things that happened through the years that change your lives for a short time, for a long time, or forever. Here are some things that have happened that changed mine:

Of course moving from one town to another will change a lot of things. The first time that I noticed this was when I was old enough to notice the change that occurred when we moved from Sweetwater, Texas to Olton, Texas. The school was the biggest change for me. Olton had great schools. In Sweetwater I had gone to a segregated school which had very poor facilities. I was really behind in my school work. When I started the sixth grade in Olton, it was really a challenge for me. It was not until the eighth grade that I began to feel more comfortable in school.

Another big changeoccurred in my work. I had always worked in the fields, either hoeing cotton or pulling cotton. I had also planted onions and picked potatoes and tomatoes. When I was a freshman in high school I got a job working in the local newspaper, *The Olton Enterprise*. Now, that was different! It was a job inside, away from the sun!! I started by cleaning the place and I was paid 45c an hour. Within a month or two I was raised to 50c an hour! Okay!

Because I was working I was able to buy my first car at age 14! That will also change you. Believe it or not, but one time at an early age I walked up to the president of the local bank and asked for $300 so I could buy a car. Mr. Bill Yates, the president of the bank, said to me, "Joe, sure, tell the teller to give you the $300 and pay them back as you can." I might explain that Mr. Yates knew me because we bowled in a bowling league together and his daughter, Oneeta, was in my high school class.

Another big change was when I graduated from high school. I was blessed that I already had a job at *The Olton Enterprise*. I had worked there part time all through high school. I had not planned on attending college. My first Christmas at The Olton Enterprise my boss Troy Martin gave me a $500.00 bonus check. Boy, that was something! It was a blessing from God. I divided the money with Dad, Mom and my brothers and sisters.

The next move was from Olton, Texas to Abilene. The move was so that I could attend college at Hardin-Simmons University. It was weird! I had always lived with Mom and Dad, and now I was living in a dormitory with all guys. I felt lonely and sad, but since I had to work to make a living, I did not have too much time to dwell on it. I would go to class in the mornings, and then to work in the afternoons. Sometimes I ate in the cafeteria and sometines I ate in my room. I had a small portable oven where I could toast some bread, or heat up some food.

The next thing that changed my life was when I got married. Wow! What a change! The first challenge was to find a place to live. I will confess that I had found this very economical place close to Hardin-Simmons, but Liandra and her sister Mary did not go for it. You see, the place was one room, and we would share a kitchen and bath with the owner of the house who was a little old lady. I thought we could make it . . . not Liandra or Mary! (Thanks, Liandra and Mary, you saved me!) They found this small garage apartment with a very small kitchen and combination bedroom and living room; with a tiny bath room and closet. We progressed to a duplex apartment which was bigger. We had a bedroom, kitchen, bath, and a small living room.

The next big change in our lives was when Liandra became pregnant. I did not know what to do. At one time the doctor told her she had to stay in bed for some days! What was all that about? Her moods changed and for no reason at all, she would cry. I would ask her, "Honey, why are you crying?" She would answer, "I don't know!"

Deaths in the family certainly change people. Of course the death of Dad and then Mother really affected me. The first death in our extended family was the Rev. Milton Martinez, husband of my oldest sister, Margarita. Milton was only 39 years of age. Mague came to live in Abilene to be close to our family. The next death was that of my nephew, James Smith, son of Jimmy and Sarah Smith. Little James had cancer and he died at the age of five. I still do not know why he had to die. Next was my baby sister, Rachel Alcorta Smith. She was 41 and had two children. I still do not know why she had to die either. But, God is sovereign and knows what He does.

Books I Have Written

While my wife and I were members at Ambler Baptist Church in Abilene, Texas, I came up with the idea of writing the history of the church in 1960. I believe every year the church would celebrate its anniversary. Our church was a mission of First Baptist Church.

We had church members to take their pictures and then I interviewed families to write their stories as to when they join and other interested information. The book is 8 ½ by 11, and I had H-SU print shop to print it.

The second book I published was a history of The Dallas Cowboys. The title in Spanish is: *La Historia de un Famoso Equipo: Los Dallas Cowboys* (A History of a Famous Team: the Dallas Cowboys), copyright date is 1989. I had become a fan of The Cowboys since their beginning in 1960. Milton Martinez, my brother-in-law, took me to see my very first Dallas Cowboys game which was played in the Cotton Bowl in Dallas. I think we paid $3.00 for each ticket.

As I became a fan, I began to read all about the team. For Christmas, my wife gave me my first Dallas Cowboy book, *Pro or Con, The Dallas Cowboys*. It really touched me because we were struggling financially, and she somehow or other had bought me that book. She continued to buy me books about the Cowboys. I also began to subscribe to *The Dallas Cowboys Weekly Newsletter*.

It was early in 1980 that I came up with the idea of writing the history of the Dallas Cowboys, but to write it in Spanish. That had not been done! I began to collect all kinds of books and articles on the team. I have a philosophy that the answer is always "No" if you do not ask. So, I got brave and called Coach Landry's office and ask if he would grant me an interview. He said "Yes!" I also got an interview with Mr. Tex Schram, general manager of The Cowboys. He was very helpful in getting much needed information and pictures for me.

I don't know if it was a policy, restriction or what, but I was not able to interview The Dallas Cowboys Cheerleaders or the sponsor. The girls were very well protected from the media. One funny story that happened when I drove up to Dallas to meet Coach Landry was the cheerleaders. As we walked into the building, my oldest son, Joe, was with me. At that same time, in the afternoon, the Cheerleaders were returning from a performance. I quickly turned to Joe, and said, "Son, where is the camera?" He said, "Dad, you have it!" Needless to say, I did not have it. We both had left it in the car. Years later, Joe was still saying that was a day he remembers, that he missed out on having his picture taken with thirty-six beautiful girls!

I typed all the stories on the Cowboys in the print shop of Hardin-Simmons University. That is really where I learned to use a computer. At that time, the print shop was one place where there was a computer. I normally would do it during my lunch hours because the employees of the shop were not using it. Billy Tucker, in charge of the print shop, helped me with all kinds of questions in formatting the book and getting it ready for print.

I had a lot of fun writing it! At that time the Cowboy organization was a class act. I received a great letter from star running back Herschel Walker. It was very exciting meeting Quarterback Roger Staubach. My only disappointment was that through those years the Cowboys did not win the Super bowl.

I was very sad and disappointed the day original owner Clint Murchison sold the Cowboys to H. R. "Bum" Bright. I was sad and angry when Mr. Bright sold the Cowboys to Jerry Jones on February, 1989. On February 25, Jerry Jones fired my hero Mr. Tom Landry.

The Cowboys book did not do well at all. First, it was in Spanish! Second, a majority of the men do not read; and third, the Cowboys did not do well on those years. And, I did not do a very good job of marketing the book.

Through the years I have taught special evening classes for bankers, nurses, doctors, lawyers, and telephone operators. I decided to write a small practical book for bankers with the name, *Essential Spanish for Bankers*. The H-SU print shop printed the books. I followed with *Essential Spanish for Doctors and Nurses*. Then I published *Essential Spanish for Policemen, Lawyers, and Judges; Essential Spanish for Teachers and Other School Personnel; Essential Spanish for Restaurant Personnel; and Essential Spanish to Share Your Faith*.

Of the above books, *Essential Spanish for Teachers and Other School Personnel* has done real well. It has helped a lot since I have given some workshops related to teaching Spanish.

In 1991 my friend Glenn Dromgoole, editor of *the Abilene Reporter-News* called me and said he wanted to offer Spanish lessons to his readers. Over a hamburger, Glenn and I decided to have one daily lesson for a period of sixty days. Glenn came up with the title: *Speak Spanish in 60 Days.*

After the 60 days were over, several people called and said, I missed lesson four or lesson ten, etc. Glenn and I decided to compile the 60 lessons into a book. We also came up with the idea of recording each lesson in a cassette. The H-SU print shop did the printing of the books.

Dr. Teresia Taylor and I recorded the lessons in the H-SU laboratory. We had a lot of fun recording. We made mistakes and laughed a lot during the recording. It was Gary Stephenson, Educational Technology Services Director who spliced the tape and corrected our mistakes. So we recorded on reel to reel, and then to cassette, and now we have a CD!

Speak Spanish in 60 Days was a great success in Abilene. In fact, in Abilene, it was the bestseller of the year! The book and tape sold for $9.95. It truly was a bargain. In the last twenty years the book has been published in Newspapers in San Antonio, Houston, Wichita Falls, and Oregon. We have sold over 7,000 copies.

Another of my books, *The Almost True Story of a Church Committee*, did not do well either. This book was based on a real life situation. I was a member of Elmcrest Baptist Church and I was elected to serve on a pulpit committee. Our job was to find and to recommend a minister for our church. The book, in a humorous form reports the work of the committee from start to finish. All the names in the book have been changed to protect the innocent!

My latest book is, *Words of Wisdom From a Cool College Professor*. This book is a collection of about sixty different essays on different topics. The essays have to do with Mother's Day, Father's Day, The Fourth of July, Christmas, Easter, etc. For about twenty years I have been guest columnist for *The Abilene Reporter-News*. Most of these essay have appeared in the newspaper.

People Who Have Influenced My Life

The cliché, "No man is an island," is certainly true. There have been many people who have influenced my life in a great way. Of course, my parents certainly did. From them I learned the basics: work hard, always tell the truth, be honest and respect people, and treat people the way you want to be treated. Certainly my two brothers and seven sisters influenced me in a great way. Liandra, my wife, continues to be a great influence on my life. She supports and encourages me. She is my greatest "fan."

Family and friends are not the only major influences. Many of my elementary, high school, and college teachers were a great influence. Mr. Fischer, Mr. and Mrs. Ford, Dr. Mason, and Dr. Ellis will always have a special place in my heart.

All the ministers where I have been a member in a church have influenced my life in different ways. Rev. Lester Vinson, at an early age gave me a nickel for every 100 I brought home from school. One day I was throwing up a candy and catching it when Bro. Ortiz came around. He told me, "Joe, how can you be playing with a piece of candy when there are hundreds of children that would love to have that candy."

Rev. Glen Godsey changed my life forever. He was my mentor, my counselor, my role model. I will miss him. Bro. Godsey modeled the true Christian life for me. As one person said in his funeral, "Bro. Godsey was Romans 12." Rev. T.C. Melton, Burtis Williams and Dr. Dale Suel at Elmcrest Baptist Church were great men. I learned much from them. Earl Garrett, a close friend of mine, has taught and helped me so much. From Earl, I learn to really be a professional person. I learned to be on time for everything! I highly respect Earl's words of wisdom as he counsels me.

My friend Glenn Dromgoole gave me an opportunity to write. Glenn made me an author! Several of my close colleagues at H-SU have influenced me. I have learned so much from my close Rotary friends. My close brothers and sisters from church have prayed for me.

Books I Recommend Reading

There are literally thousands of excellent books written in the market. Reading books broadens your horizons, and helps an individuals to look at things in a different way. Books teach, encourage, entertain and help individuals to be better people.

To encourage students to read and do better in school I wrote the following article about reading as a guest columnist for *The Abilene Reporter-News*:

A Good Reader Can Be A Good Leader

School will soon start again! There have been studies made as why some students drop out of school and fail. My belief is that many students are not really interested in receiving a traditional classroom education. Most of these students certainly want the benefits of an education but they are not willing to work at it.

My second idea as to why students fail is their home environment. I am a firm believer that "everything" good begins at home. When both Mom and Dad encourage education their children will learn.

My third idea is the topic of this essay: not reading. There is not enough room to explain the benefits of good reading. The most important thing in pre-school, kindergarten, first and second grade should be reading. Parents and teachers should do everything possible to teach children how to read. Then after children learn to read, keep them reading and reading!!!

Every summer I bribe my grandchildren into reading. Here is the deal: You receive $5.00 for each book (100 pages or more) you read. I want the title of the book, the author, and three good sentences about the book. Last summer I paid $200.00 to Morgan and Jessica.

Encourage your children to read the newspaper, magazines, and simple recipes. Have them read in their interest. Take them to the library. Tell them, "One hour of TV or video games, one hour of reading!" Children generally do what they see their parents doing not necessarily what the parents say. So, parents, how many times has your son/daughter caught you reading a book?

Parents, do you need suggestions for some good books? Here are just a few. Everyone needs to read these two books: *How to Win Friends and Influence People*, and *How to Stop Worrying and Start Living* by Dale Carnegie. Are you in business or in sales, then you need to read: *The Magic of Thinking Big* by David Schwartz.

Do you want to succeed in what you do? Zig Zigglar, the master of enthusiasm has several. The two I recommend are: *See You at the Top* and *Over The Top*. Another good one is *Go For The Magic* by former general manager of the Orlando magic, Pat Williams.

All parents need to read: *How to Make Children Mind Without Losing Yours, Dare to Discipline,* How *to Have a New Kid by Friday, Bringing up Boys,* and *Bringing up Girls.*

Has your son/daughter gone astray? You need to read *Stick a Geranium in Your Hat and Be Happy* by Barbara Johnson.

Are you engaged or married? These two books are indispensible: *His Needs, Her Needs* by Willard F. Harley; and *The Five Love Languages* by Gary D. Chapman.

Do you want to be rich? *The One Minute Millionaire* by Mark Victor Hansen and Robert G. Allen is a great one. Another one is *The Blessed Life* by Robert Morris.

Do you want to be healthy and fit? There are hundreds of books on this topic. A big authority on this subject is Dr. Kenneth H. Cooper. Thousands consult with him. A very simple one and lots of fun to read is *Look Great Feel Great* by Joyce Meyer. Want to begin jogging/running? Then read, *Galloway's Book On Running* by Jeff Galloway.

Cannot get along with your in-laws or your boss? *The DNA of Relationships* by Gary Smalley is great.

Need help in praying? Try Philip Yancey's book, *Prayer.*

Do you like sports? There are thousands of books on this subject. Three of my favorite ones are *Landry, the Legend and the Legacy* by Bob St. John; *Jack Nicklaus: My Story* by Ken Bowden; and *They Call Me Coach* by John Wooden.

Of course, the book to read is the Bible. The Bible has sixty-six books and they are all full of good Godly wisdom. If you are in a rush, just read Jesus' Sermon on the Mount, found in Matthew, chapters 5, 6, and 7; or read Jesus' instructions to his disciplines as He is leaving earth: John, chapter 14, 15, and 16. If you read, study, and apply these six chapters to your life, you will never be the same.

Okay, parents, teachers, and students, let us get to reading. Turn off your cell phone and TV. Reading will open many doors to the unknown. Reading can take you on that vacation you have never taken, or it can literally open another world for you. Reading is like golf, chess, dancing, or running. The more you do it, the better you get at it!

Other books I would recommend: *Quiet Strength* by Tony Dungy; *Landry, the Legend and the Legacy* by Bob St. John; *What Every Man Wants in a Woman, and What Every Woman Wants in a Man*; *Rekindled* by Pat and Jill Williams; author of *Love and Respect* by Emerson Eggerichs; *Who Moved my Cheese*; *Become a Better You* by Joel Osteen; *When God Doesn't Make Sense* by Dr. James Dobson;

Raising A Modern-Day Knight by Robert Lewis; *A Man's Guide to the Spiritual Disciplines* by Patrick Morley; *My Utmost for His highest* an updated edition in today's language by Oswald Chambers; and *Man to Man* by Charles R. Swindoll

I would certainly recommend the books of Charles Stanley, Chuck Swindoll, Billy Graham, David Jeremiah, Max Lucado, Beth Moore, Joyce Meyer, John C. Maxwell, John McArthur, Rick Warren, James Dobson, and Patrick Morley,

Things I Would Like to Tell My Guests in My Home

(But I Never Do!)

1. No alcohol of any kind in the house is permitted.
2. No smoking!
3. No cussing in the house!!!
4. Small children (13 and under) are to eat in the kitchen or in the dining room, and on a table.
5. After you or your children finish eating please take dirty dishes to the kitchen sink. It will be appreciated!!!
6. In the shower, the water will be turned off after 5 minutes!
7. No nasty movies are to be shown in the house!
8. If you are here on Sunday morning plan on going to church somewhere
9. Please don't complain that the house is too cold or too hot!!! (Propane and electricity are very expensive!)
10. Helping to wash the dishes after a meal is much appreciated!
11. If you use the potty, please do not put tissue in the commode; place tissue in the waste basket!
12. If you use the house phone (portable) please put it back where you got it!
13. If you are upstairs please be quiet . . . . walk softly!!
14. There are lights switches . . . please turn off the light switch when you leave the room. Nickels and dimes add to dollars!
15. The TV remote is to stay in the TV room!!! Real close to the television. (Keep the sound low!!!)

16. Children are to be seen, not heard!!! No running in the house—running is outside!! Throwing a ball inside the house of any kind is a "No! No!"
17. No dogs or cats inside the house!!!
18. We prefer to visit with you instead of watching TV.
19. My wife and I love for our family and friends to visit us. You honor us with your presence.

Family Conflicts

Every family in the world has challenges, difficulties, and problems. That is part of family living. But, the differences in families are how the challenges, difficulties and problems are handled. In the next few pages I am relating two true stories of families who I know in the hope that some family members will learn from them and try hard not to make the same mistakes. (I have changed the names and towns so not to embarrass anyone)

The Felix and Barbara Smith Family

Felix Smith and Barbara were married in Brownwood, Texas, December, 1962. They made their home in Dallas, Texas. Felix was a barber and Barbara was a hair dresser and later became a registered nurse. For a long time they lived 2101 at Canyon Street in Dallas. Felix and Barbara adopted their daughter Gina; later Barbara gave birth to their only son Fernando. The family was members of First Baptist Church.

Something happened during the years when Gina and Fernando were in middle school. Gina began to bring boys home while the parents were not around. Fernando began to run around with the wrong crowd. Gina got pregnant and she had an abortion. She quit school and married a Black man by the name of Wendell. From this marriage they had two children, Sarah and David.

Gina divorced Wendell and then had two other sons, Daniel and John. Felix and Barbara adopted John so they could provide insurance and other needs for him. John always considered Felix and Barbara as his parents; He did know that Gina was his birth mother.

Gina now lives with Jim who she has been with for several years. Jim is a hardworking man. Gina also works. Gina has a big bad foul mouth and this has been passed on to Fernando's children since they are around her many times.

Fernando began to live with Yvonne and together they had five children. They never married; Yvonne had a daughter by a previous marriage. Fernando began to be in and out of jail for different things.

Fernando and Barbara purchased two houses and passed them on to Fernando and Gina. They also helped them by buying them cars. Fernando and Barbara continued to pay taxes and repairs on the houses.

Fernando and Barbara encouraged Fernando and Gina to go to school but they did not want an education.

In 2000, Fernando and Barbara bought a brand new house for themselves, Fernando asked for the house on Canyon Street. Fernando and Barbara permitted Fernando and Yvonne to live on Canyon Street free of rent. Many times the water, electricity, etc. was caught off because Fernando and Yvonne did not pay the bills. When Fernando and Yvonne were arrested the house was trashed. It was in very bad conditions and Barbara had to repair the house so it could be rented.

 In 2007, the worst happened: Fernando and his wife were sent to prison for dealing in drugs. Both were given about 12 years. At the writing of this book, Fernando is in prison and Yvonne is in a half-way house ready to be turned loose.

Fernando and Barbara took the children in when their parents were sent to prison. The baby boy, Richard, was born in prison. Fernando suddenly died on March, 2009, and that left Barbara all alone to take care of the children. Fernando did not want to take care of the children and he told that to Barbara

At this time Barbara is sixty-nine years of age and in failing health. At present she is working as a school nurse at Panthor High School. We do not know how she does it, but she takes the children to day care and to school. She alone does the cooking, cleaning, and washing, etc.

Fernando has pressured Barbara to take in Yvonne when she gets to come home. We might add that the relationship between Barbara and Yvonne has never been good. At one time, Yvonee came to Barbara home and "cussed" her out. As in many families, Fernando and Barbara had bailed out Fernando and Gina many times.

Melody, Fernando's oldest daughter, graduated from high school, but she is already given grandma Barbara lots of problems. In 2010, Melody wanted her freedom so she just got up and left the house without telling Barbara. Well, as we all know, life is hard out there and Melody returned because she could not make it with her relatives and friends. Melody was supposed to have enrolled in college (Sept., 2010), but she said her scores on the ACT were late to be reported to that university.

Well, Melody left Barbara's home again this year (2010) around November. She is working at a pizza shop.

Reader, do you get the picture? Many people want privileges and goodies but without responsibilities! Something went wrong. Fernando and Barbara provided for their children, but in no way should they be totally responsible for their grandchildren.

The Family of Beto and Melena Jones

Melena, married the Rev. Manuel Martinez in Hart, Texas. Melena gave birth to her oldest son, John Jones; and then they adopted Pedro. Manuel died at a very young age of thirty-nine in Mercedes, Texas. Melena and the two sons moved to Sweetwater, Texas to be close to family. The two boys gave Melena a very hard time. Melena married Benito Rangel and they moved to Houston, Texas.

Pedro joined the military and then was discharged because of drugs. Pedro married Fina Esquivel and they had two children: Pedro and Marisol Helena. Pedro and family lived with Benito and Melena for a long time. Benito and Melena helped Pedro in many ways, especially in trying to get him to work and pay bills.

Benito was a good solid Christian man and he tried to help Melena with the boys by teaching them how to become men. After Benito died of cancer, Melena married Beto Gray. Beto has encouraged Melena to let Pedro and Alicia handle their own financial problems.

Beto and Melena sold their house, which originally belonged to Benito, with the idea that Pedro and Alicia would find their own place. Beto and Melena purchased a smaller home.

A few years ago, Pedro divorced Fina and married Alicia Montez (a Mexican girl from Mexico). They have one boy, David born August 29, 1998. Lately (2010) Pedro Gutierrez, grandson of Melena, came to live with Beto and Melena. Not only that, but Pedro is married and they have a child!

Beto called me in November to tell me that he wanted to move to an assistant living place. The problem was Melena. She did not want to go because the grandson is living with them. Beto wants to sell the house and that way they could have some funds for help. Melena wants to leave the house to Pedro ! I told Beto, sell the house!!! If Pedro wants the house, then he must be willing to buy the house at a fair price.

John graduated from college in Houston and he married Benita Lara who is also a college graduate. They had four children: Reyna, Santiago, Rachel, and Blanca. John and Benita have always managed their finances real well. Benita home-schooled all her children and all are doing very well in school. In fact, two children have graduated from Texas A&M.

But before John became a school teacher he was working in a telephone company and there he had an extramarital affair. After the affair, there was reconciliation. Later Benita lost her mother, and her Dad re-married. The re-marriage by the dad was not accepted by the family.

So, what is the problem? Well, Beto and Melena, mostly Melena is still helping Pedro and his family with money. From Melena's Social Security check comes the payment of Pedro and Alicia's house. Melena is so simple and so giving that she does not know how to say, "No!" To top it off, Alicia does not get along or respect Melena, her mother-in-law.

Add to the above to let you know that the children of John and Benita do not know their grandmother Melena. For some reason or other they have stayed away! Many times Melena had to call John and Benita to see if she could come over and visit! Seldom do John and Benita go and visit Melena and Beto.

Reyna has married Johnny Hayseed and now they have a daughter. Well that little great-granddaughter has never visited her great-grandma Melena. Why? I realize that somewhere along the line there has been broken relationships between Pedro, Alicia, John, Benita, Beto and Melena. Regardless, some of these differences need to be put aside and the families need to come together for some good fellowships. Cousins need to know and respect each other.

I believe people soon forget where they came from. Many simply do not appreciate the hard work of their parents. Some children obtain a little education or come to some money and they quickly forget where they came from. It is sad that Melena cannot count on her sons to help her out a little. Many times Melena needs a ride and her two sons are not available. As a college professor, I often tell my students, "You may not want to see your grandparents, but your grandparents do want to see you!"

Vacations We Have Taken

Vacations are fun! Vacations are for family members to rest, relax and get refreshed from work. Here are a few vacations we have taken together:

Twin Lakes, Colorado

For about twenty years our family vacationed in Twin Lakes, Colorado. The reason? Well, my place of employment, Hardin-Simmons University, purchased these cabins in the mountains of Colorado. Our cost was $5.00 per night! Not bad!

Liandra, Cecilia, Joe, Adriel, Andrew, and I vacationed in this beautiful place. Our first year was really an experience. As we travelled from hot climate Abilene toward New Mexico, there was a change of weather. As we passed Raton Pass, New Mexico and into Colorado we decided to stop and enjoy the mountain view. Wow! It was freezing cold! We could not believe it! But, Liandra was prepared and the jackets quickly came out.

Twin Lakes is located about 125 miles West from Denver, Colorado, and about 15 miles from Leadville, an old mining town. There was a Safeway store in Leadville that we would go and purchase our groceries. In town we did the laundry and a little shopping.

The first thing was to buy our fishing license. That first year the fishing license was either $5.00 or $10 for a three day period. I would take the boys trout fishing in the two lakes of Twin Lakes. After two or three days we would have a fish fry.

It was very cold at night and in the early morning; around noon it was very pleasant. It is a beautiful scene from the cabin toward the mountains and the lakes. The boys and I explored walking up the mountain. During the day after lunch if it was not too cold we would go swimming.

One year we had a big scare with Andrew! We lost him! We all got in the car and drove down to the lake and looked and looked. About three hours later as we are driving back to the cabin, he meets us climbing up to the cabin. His first words, "Hey, guys, where have you been, I have been looking for you!" We could have killed him!! He had worried us so much.

Of course we would explore driving in different directions. A couple of times we drove up to Aspen which is a rich tourist place. Everything is so expensive. The drive is dangerous because one has to drive through the mountains and it is very scary!

We found another lake which we enjoyed very much by the name of Cottonwood Lake up in the mountains. It was good for fishing and picnics. After four or five days we would drive up to Arvada, Colorado, to spend a couple of days with our friends, Rudy and Betty Morado. Liandra and I had worked with Rudy and Betty as young people back in our mission in Abilene. They had married and because of Rudy's work they had moved to Colorado. Rudy had help to build Casa Bonita, a beautiful Mexican restaurant. Rudy did so much for the restaurant. He developed different entertainment things one could do. He built a scene where a gorilla comes out and attacks a man, and the man to flee jumps into a big pool of water. Then he did the two dancing people where it was really one person dancing. The food was really good, and the service was excellent. It was the first time I had seen that by raising of a flag at your table the waiters would come and ask you what else was needed. There was also a place where families could have their picture taken. There were different costumes that one could choose for pictures.

Rudy and Betty also took us to eat pizza at the Organ Grinder. It was an awesome place. It was a great place for entertainment for the children. One year, Rudy, Betty and family came out to Twin Lakes for some fishing. Another year our family went with Rudy, Betty and their family to a church camp in Nebraska.

On Sunday mornings, we would go with the Morado family to church. In the afternoon different church members went to the park for games and a picnic. It was really good fellowship. On Monday mornings, our family sadly would drive back to Abilene, Texas.

Cistern Bay, Wisconsin

When Liandra was a teenager, her family would go from Breckenridge, Texas, to Cistern Bay, Wisconsin, for the cherry harvest. Liandra's dad was like a foreman or a manger who got the cherry grove ready for the pickers. They did this for several years. Liandra, Cecilia, Joe, and I travelled to Wisconsin twice. On our way we stopped at Chicago to visit with our uncle Porfirio Solis. Liandra really enjoyed the family showing them the place where they stayed and the fields where they worked.

I remember going to the museum of the Green Bay Packers. We normally would go in the summer but the water was still too cold for swimming. I remember one year at a park we rented a bicycle for two.

Acapulco, Mexico

One year, Mario and Irene Garcia, Liandra and I drove to Mexico City. Mexico City is an awesome city. It is very modern and there are so many things to do. When in the city we always attend the National Folkloric Dance. The many dances of the history of Mexico are tremendous. The dresses of the women are so colorful. Another place we visit is Xochimilco, the floating gardens with its beautiful flowers and greenery.

Well, since we were young and full of enthusiasm, and a little crazy, someone asked, "Hey, how far is it to Acapulco from here?" No one knew, so we said, "Let's find out!" And we did. That night after finding a motel, we went to a nice restaurant to eat. The next day as we were getting into the car, we noticed that the license plates to our car were gone! Well, we found out that we probably parked in a wrong place or we had gotten a fine for some parking violation. The next thing was to find city hall and go pay the fine so we could get the tags back. It took a long time but we found it and paid the ten pesos fine!

The water was beautiful in Acapulco. I remember that on the next day when we wanted to buy swim suits we could not because everyone was taking their siesta! The siesta in Acapulco was between 2:00 and 4:00 p.m.

One exciting thing that happened as we were driving back from Acapulco was running into a cow. I was driving pretty fast because we wanted to get to the next town before it got dark. As we were driving Liandra hollers to me, "Joe, there is something crossing the road." By the time I slam on the brakes I had hit a cow. Mario and Irene were asleep in the back, and they got up asking, "What happened?" Liandra said, "Oh, nothing, Joe just hit a cow!"

We were scared that we would get in trouble and we quickly left the scene. I think the cow was alive and had moved on. I also was very worried about Mario's new car. Luckily it did not damage the radiator enough for water to leak out. Mario had the car fixed back in Garland.

It is a lot of fun to travel with Mario because he loves to eat! When he buys something, he always asks, "Does anyone want something?" Mario is a great guy and he never minds paying for everyone. He has a big heart. Mario has made a lot of money in his fence building business.

Mexico City

One year Liandra and I took three couples on vacation with us to Mexico City. Flying with us were Fred and Benita Stokes, Sammy and Anita Alcorta, and Mario and Irene Garcia. We flew airline Mexicana from Dallas to Mexico City.

Now in my old age I have learned to take it easy during vacation time. One big mistake I made with the couples is that the first night we landed in Mexico City I pushed them too much. That night I went and got tickets for the Folkloric show. We all went but most of us were tired and sleepy. The next morning I believe it was Sammy and Anita that got sick. A doctor had to come to the hotel room to check them out.

I remember we went to see and climb the Pyramids of the Sun and the Moon. I had this game going with the couple: the first couple that got mad with his/her spouse would buy dinner for the other three couples. I think Sammy and Anita lost! At the pyramids, Anita liked this Mexican dress and wanted to buy it. Naturally, she asked Sammy what he thought. Sammy responded like a man, "If you like it buy it." Well that was not what Anita wanted to hear. But I don't remember if they bought us dinner or not!

Ruidoso, New Mexico

H-SU sold the cabins in Colorado and later bought cabins in Ruidoso, New Mexico. The cost was $35 per night and later went up to $45 per night. We have been at the New Mexico cabins two or three times. The cabins are about 10 miles out of town. We learned that we cannot boil beans in Ruidoso! So, now, we cook our beans in Abilene before we go there!

We have had many adventures at the cabins. We normally play cards at night, sleep late, and have a good breakfast. We then drove into town for sightseeing and shopping. A couple of times we have vacationed with our son Joe and his family. Joe and I enjoy playing golf in the beautiful golf courses. Amber and Liandra love the many shopping places in town. Morgan and Jessica enjoy feeding the deer who come up to the cabins. One year, Michel Castillo joined the group and that year it snowed. It was fun having a snow ball fight. Michael and the two girls, Jessica and Morgan had fun sliding down the hill. Michael had a make-shift snow sled. One year Joe drove us up to the highest mountain in Ruidoso. It was exciting and a little scary for the altitude and the curves on the road.

Madrid, Spain (the year 2000)

This was not really a vacation but a university sabbatical for me. Hardin-Simmons University paid for my part but I had to pay for the travel and lodging expenses for Liandra and our son Andrew who also went with us. I believe it was a 14 hour flight.

The idea for me was to personally know more about the culture of the Spanish people, and places of which language I had been teaching for a long time. It was very exciting to personally visit the home where Miguel de Cervantes author of Don Quixote had lived.

We had the opportunity to mix and mingle with the people to hear their language spoken. We were blessed that some Baptist missionaries in Spain took us in and showed around Spain. The Henrys whose daughter and son I had taught at Hardin-Simmons were the friendly missionaries. We learned so much from them. Two or three times I was given the opportunity to speak in their churches.

One Saturday they took us on a family picnic up in the mountains of Madrid. It was an all-day affair. First, the driving! My wife and Andrew cannot take the fast driving and the altitude. They often had to take Dramamine. It helps if they ride in the front seat of the car. What families prepare is paella. Every family has their own recipe. Wood is gathered and a fire is started. After lunch many took a siesta.

One day we took a bus trip to visit the coast of Spain. There our son, Andrew, got to see the first topless women at the beach. It is a custom!!! In the long bus run we were very disturbed because of the cigarette smoking. Get this . . . the front of the bus, no smoking, but a person could smoke in the back of the bus!

In Spain we stayed in a dormitory that was used for seminary students. Since it was summer, we had it all to ourselves. There were no air conditioners! If Liandra and I got hot, we went to the basement.

We learned that the Spanish people go to bed very late. Their supper is around 9:00 or 10:00 p.m. So, many times we joined the Spanish people for midnight walks around town and the plaza. We felt very safe. Everything was so expensive that we could not afford to buy anything as far as souvenirs. The food was also expensive. In the city we were surprised to see so many young people smoking.

The Spanish culture is very different from ours. In church we soon got accustomed to the Spanish greeting of hugging and kissing on both cheeks when you meet someone and when you say goodbye.

Some Changes That I Have Seen in my Life Time

I would like to share some things that I have seen change during my 71 years of life. It would be impossible for me to name or list every change that has happened during my life time, but permit me to share just a few.

The good old **TELEPHONE**. Our family had its first telephone in 1952. Imagine that. So when we lived in Mexico and in Sweetwater we did not have a telephone in our house. Now, that first telephone was black in color, in fact, they were all black! Later we had red and green phones. Most telephones in those days were party lines; in other words, sometimes you could hear what other people were saying. (That was fun! . . . until they would tell you to get off the line!) A person would have to wait a while until a person got off that line so you could use it. The numbers one dialed were in a rotary circle form.

Telephone answering machines are rather recent. Today we enjoy cellular telephones which can be used anywhere in the world. These modern cellular telephones can be simple or they can be sophisticated depending on how much the customer wants to pay.

Whoever heard of a person being able to watch his/her favorite sports team play on their cell phone? Another click and a person can know the weather in Chicago! Another click and that cell phone tells you how to go to New York City!

How about the **TELEVISION**? Our first black and white TV arrived in our home around 1954. We were lucky if we could get two channels from Lubbock, Texas. Now there are dozens and dozens of TV stations.

Sports, weather, movies, you name it, you got it! And, the channels went off at midnight.

Who remembers the **TYPEWRITER**? In high schools typing classes were offered. In case you are thirty or younger, I will try to describe it to you. A typewriter was a manual machine which had keys with the letters backwards. There was a printed keyboard (similar to today's computer's keyboard) on front and a person learned where the keys were. You would learn to "press" or "hit" the key you wanted and it would print on the piece of paper you had inserted into the typewriter. After the manual typewriter came the electric typewriter which was easier and faster to operate. A first year student had to type 40 words per minute to earn an "A" in the class. A second year student had to type 60 or more. I enjoyed these classes, and I am thankful that even today I can put that knowledge to work.

In school and in business the **MIMOGRAPH MACHINE** was very useful. My first year teaching at Brownwood Junior High I had to learn how to use the mimeograph machine to make copies for exams or other handouts. A person would have to cut (type) a stencil on a black carbon sheet with a typewriter. Then the stencil was placed around a cylinder and by hand you would turn a handle to make some copies. How many teachers out there remember this great instrument?

Then came the **Xerox machine**! Wow! That was a blessing! Of course the Xerox machine has been improved so much that a person can do so many things with it. The machine now can print front and back of a sheet and the machine will collate and staple for you. Something related now is the **FAX machine**; one click and your letter or business form is miles away!

How about the **AUTOMOBILE**? The first car that I remember in our house was a 1939 Chevrolet. Next we upgraded to a 1941 Chevrolet. Both cars were black and standard gear shift. The cost of the cars was probably less than $1500. When I married Liandra I was driving a 1955 two-tone Chevrolet. Our first ever brand-new car was a 1965 Chevy Impala. Wow! Today, thanks to our God, we are blessed with a 2009 Camary valued at around $25,000. The Ford, Chevrolet, and the Cadillac were very popular cars. Now there are hundred to choose from. It is unbelievable.

How about the **PRICES** of things? All things have gone up! Coffee use to be 5 cents! What do you think about the following prices?

1950-60		2000 to 2011
5c	Coca Cola	50c to $2.00
16c	loaf of bread	1.00 to 3.00
5c	cup of coffee	1.00 to 2.50
9c	movies	5.00 to 8.00
5c	pop corn	50c to 3.00
25c	a hamburger	1.00 to 5.00
16c	gallon, gas	2.39-3.39
25c	hair cut	7.00 – 12.00
5c	ice cream cone	1.25 – 2.59
39c	gallon, milk	2.00 – 4.00

Hair styles for men and women were pretty normal. Men wore short hair, while women wore long hair. Now days, everything seems acceptable. Color or length is personal preference.

Style in clothes has changed a lot. It seems to me that men's clothing is pretty traditional and simple, while the women's clothes have had many changes. The mini skirt is still in style, and now we have the mini blouse where the mid-drift can be seen.

I believe men dress because it is a necessity. Women dress to please men and to compete with other women. A woman always asks her husband, "How do I look?" How many times, will a husband ask his wife, "How do I look?" On Easter Sunday, look around your church. Who has the new clothes? It is the women and the little girls! The men still wear last year's suit!

Dress in churches has changed a lot. A lot of so called "Modern Churches" are accepting all kinds of casual dress in church. In "My church" I have seen women with shorts, tight pants, blue jeans, low cut blouses, and no shoes. If my Mother was to see these women dressed like that, she would pass out!

Changes in Sports. Most schools offered football, basketball, and baseball for boys. Football was most popular. For the girls, schools offered basketball and volleyball. That was it. Today, by law, schools have to offer the above sports, plus tennis, softball, and swimming. And not only that, but the government says equal time, space, and money has to be spent on girls as they do boys!

In college there are Division I, Division II, and Division III. Why? Well the size of the school and the size of the budget. In the 60s one could attend a sporting event for a dollar or two. Today, bowl games start at $100 and go up to $700 a game! That is ridicules! Suppose a university has 70,000 in attendance and each customer pays $100; that equals to $7,000,000. Where does that money go?

The professional teams are worse! The owners sometimes pay their players into the millions! In my opinion, no football, basketball, or baseball player is worth a million dollars to see.

I am not smart enough to know all the answers to inflation. However, I would recommend that the things that are "not essential" do not buy them! Examples: Cokes and sporting events. Walk more, drive less. Down size in everything.

Win the Battle of the Bulge

Many Americans find themselves daily fighting the battle of the bulge. About two thirds of the population of the United States is overweight. Why? The answer seems simple: People love to eat more than they like to exercise.

The traditional American way of eating does not help the overweight person. Eating bacon and eggs, buttered toast, fried chicken, sandwiches, French fries, hot dogs, pizza, apple pie and ice cream does not help the overweight person.

Many programs offer fast ways of losing weight. Many of these work for a while, but then the weight comes back. Why? Because there is no easy way of losing weight. It takes lots of work and discipline to lose pounds and to keep them off permanently.

The real key to losing weight and keeping it off involves changing one's eating habits on a permanent basis, and to exercise at least four or five times a week. Most people know that one needs to eat a well-balanced meal, to rest properly and to exercise.

Dear reader, if you take interest in losing a few pounds, I suggest the following:

- Visit your family doctor and inform him that you desire to lose weight.
- Begin the day by eating a healthy breakfast, such as cereal, low-fat milk, toast and fruit. Keep away from bacon, ham, sausage and butter.
- During the day drink at least eight glasses of water, and keep away from junk snacks, including sodas, chips, and sweets. For lunch and supper eat a well-balanced meal: lean meat, vegetables and fruit. Try not to eat anything after 7 p.m.

- Little by little try to do away with salt and sugar in your meals. Learn to drink tea and coffee without sugar. Keep away from fried foods.
- Do not miss breakfast, even if it means just a glass of juice and toast. Breakfast is the most important meal of the day. If you want to skip a meal, skip the evening meal.
- Be realistic in setting your goal of the number of pounds you want to shed. Set a goal of losing a pound per week rather than setting a goal of losing 10 pounds in 10 days.
- Now comes the real hard stuff: Exercise! Immediately one asks the question: What kind of exercise? You must select some exercise you enjoy; if not, you will not continue the exercise for long. Walking is an excellent exercise, but you must walk briskly as if trying to catch a plane. Jogging or running will accomplish the same thing a lot quicker. Twenty minutes to an hour five days a week will accomplish your goal.
- Your greatest enemy to exercise equals your front door. Do away with excuses such as "I don't have time," "I will get too cold," "I will get too hot" and "It is too late." You can always make these excuses.
- Begin your exercise program gradually. You might have to start by walking a couple of blocks on a daily basis, and then perhaps within three to six months, you could walk a mile. Most people can walk a mile comfortably in fifteen to twenty minutes. Walking one to two miles four or five times a week sets an ideal goal.
- You will need a good pair of walking shoes. Select a pair with flexible soles that cushion the bottom of the foot and absorb shock for the rest of the body.
- If you walk with a friend, you will enjoy the exercise more.

Walking, Jogging, Running

The big secret to walking, jogging, and running involves starting SLOW! The next thing to remember is CONSISTENCY! Probably the next thing I recommend is ACCOUNTABILITY to someone for your exercise. PRAYER always helps! Now, you need some good walking or running shoes, and a pair of shorts. Now you can begin!

Tell yourself that you can walk or jog three or four times a week. Don't say, "I will run or jog every day," because you cannot do it. Mentally you will feel better if you only accomplish one or two days a week. If you complete the three and four days a week, you will feel proud of yourself.

Remember, start SLOW! Your age, weight, and fitness will also depend on where you start or what you do the very first day. Begin your exercise by walking one quarter of a mile, or one lap around a running track. If you feel good and comfortable, walk a half a mile, or two laps around a track. Or you can begin by walking five to ten minutes every other day. Do this for about two or three months.

After three months if you still feel good and comfortable, add a little jogging. Walk a little, jog a little. Walk a few minutes, jog a few minutes. Don't push it!! Slowly keep working until you can walk and jog for a mile. Continue doing this for about three months.

When you can easily walk or jog for about twenty-two minutes you have arrived! Most doctors and trainers will tell you that about twenty-two minutes of a good work out three or four times a week helps your body to stay fit.

If you still feel good, you may want to work on increasing the time that you walk or jog. Just add a little walking or jogging to your schedule. One day get adventurous and jog or run and time yourself for either half-mile or a mile. Remember, Roger Bannister broke the four minute mile back a few years ago. So, most good athletes can run a mile in six minutes or less. You are not an athlete!! As an adult, with age, kids and stress, if you can complete a mile between nine minutes and fourteen minutes you have arrived!!!! And when that day comes, go and celebrate by buying yourself that chocolate sundae you always wanted! You deserve it!

I Ran A Marathon—26 Miles, 385 Yards!

As an adult, I have practiced running for over thirty-five years. In high school I could never participate in sports because I always had a job after school. I did not start running until after I married and had two children. A local sports writer for *The Abilene Reporter News*, clearly out of shape, reported in his column that he had gone running during the weekend and that he had completed a mile in thirteen minutes. I said to myself, "Joe, you can also run a mile and maybe run it faster!" I did! My first time, I accomplished a total time of eleven minutes! Wow! Remember, Roger Bannister broke the four minute mile back a few years ago. So, most good athletes can run a mile in six minutes or less.

So, I continued jogging off and on. One day, again, I saw in the newspaper that a local judge and a friend of mine, Jorge Solis, had run half a marathon. I said to myself, "Joe, you can probably do that!" And, I did.

One year my wife and I camped at Camp Mt Lebanon in Dallas, Texas, with a group of teenagers. "Red", the camp administrator and a long time runner, told me, "Joe, if you run a marathon, it will change your life. You will feel like a completely different person." I took Red's challenge and began training to run the Dallas White Rock Marathon. I found a book on marathon running which contained some suggestions for twelve weeks before running the marathon. The author assumes a person feels comfortable running for some length of time. He made the following recommendations:

Week one and two: Run four miles on Monday, six on Tuesday, four on Wednesday, and six on Thursday. Rest on Friday and do a long run of eight to ten miles on Saturday or Sunday. A person must also do some speed work, running hard several times around a track field during the twelve weeks as well as hill running.

People in training continue increasing little by little the miles you run during the weeks, and you also increase your long runs on Saturday or Sunday. A goal of completing three or four long runs, fifteen to twenty-two miles, comes highly recommended. Of course, eating and resting are very important.

George Solis and I worked together to run The Dallas White Rock Marathon. On Saturday mornings, George and I would do our long runs. We did anything from 10 miles to 22 miles. It helps when you run with someone.

A person has to be a "little crazy" to run a marathon! But crossing the finish line feels great! My best time in a marathon has been three hours and forty-five minutes at the age of fifty. Not bad! With the Lord's help I have continued jogging even up to my age of seventy. Walking, jogging, or running does great things for your body and your mind. It is a great stress reliver! I highly recommend it!

On October 30, 2010, (at age 71) I ran a half-marathon in 2 hours and fifty-five minutes. A year ago, I ran the local Steamboat half-marathon in 2 hours and forty-six minutes (it is very hilly!)

My best times in early years in a 5K was twenty-two minutes and fifteen seconds; forty-eight minutes in a 10K; and 1 hour and forty-five minutes in the half marathon.

Encouragement from My Students

Everyone needs a pat on the back. At work it is easy to criticize your fellow workers, but it is harder to give them a good word of encouragement.

I am including some of these letters from my students which they wrote on their own **AFTER** they had left my classes. It probably seems like bragging, but the fact is, no one really knows how a person really is unless you spend a lot of time with that person. Of course, I also realize that these letters are "personal opinions" of these students.

Regardless, I want to say thank you to the hundreds of students who have encouraged me in person and by writing some notes or letters to me.

October 15, 1975

Mr. Alcorta,

I know that you might think this a little strange. However, I once read an article about a man who when he wanted to express a thank you or an appreciation he would write a short note rather than blow it off. I guess that's kind of what I am doing.

Mr. Alcorta, you have truly impressed me and in the short time I was in your class, before I got hurt, I could see Jesus shining through you in a tremendous way. It's not every day, even on a Christian campus, that you see such concern for the students and their relationship with our Lord.

Lord willing, I will be back at HS-U in January. I know the Lord has a purpose for my having to drop out and if I open myself to His will He will use me.

Thanks again for shining Jesus love to your students.

Respectfully,
Marla Marble

Towson, MD 21204
September 1, 2009

Dr. Alcorta,

I wanted to send this note to thank you for what you did for me during summer school. It will not be forgotten and I will "pay it forward."

Sincerely,
Hannah and Best Denton

February 22, 2011

Dr. Alcorta,

Over the weekend, I was reading profile essays written by my freshmen composition students at McMurry and ran across one that mentioned a grandfather who teaches Spanish at Hardin-Simmons University. I thought, "Could that be my Mr. Alcorta from Abilene High School?" On Monday, I asked Raul Castillo if his grandfather was Dr. Joe Alcorta, and to my pleasant surprise, he said, "Yes!" I told him that I knew you way back when you were fresh out of college and teaching silly high school girls at Abilene High School.

I remember so many wonderful things about having you as a teacher. When you discovered during my senior year that I was engaged to marry shortly after graduation, you cautioned me to be very careful. Luckily, I had chosen the right guy because we have now been married forty-two years, have a wonderful thirty-six year old son, and a beautiful thirteen-year-old granddaughter.

You were also the only teacher who ever told me that I could do anything I set my mind to. I think you sensed that I came from family that didn't know how to encourage me or help me attain anything beyond the minimum. With your encouragement and that of my husband, I graduated from H-SU with bachelor's and master's degrees. I even taught your wife in an English class when I was a graduate assistant. Now I have the pleasure of teaching your grandson.

Isn't life amazing? Along our paths, we meet many people that keep reappearing to teach us the value of relationship and paying forward the blessings others have given us. I know teaching is a calling so much more than a job, and I learned that from you.

Thank you so much for being an inspiration in my life. I hope that I've done the same for as many students as you have.

Nancy Patrick, English Instructor
McMurry University
Abilene, Texas 79697

Trinity High School
February 23, 2005

Hola Dr. Alcorta,

Espero que se encuentre bien. Aquí estoy todavía en Trinity High School de maestra de español. Mi hermana está en su clase de noche. Me dio mucho gusto que usted todavía está en Hardin-Simmons. No sé si mi hermana le platico que yo comencé un grupo de hispanos aquí, y estoy ayudándoles a seguir sus sueños e ir a una universidad. Yo he escrito una carta que quiero mandarles a Hardin-Simmons para pedirles ayuda financiera para estos estudiantes pero no sé a quién mandársela. Me puede dar una recomendación?

Gracias por su ayuda,
Mónica Z. Ubillus
Foreign Language, Trinity High School

Abilene Christian University
Abilene, Texas
March 11, 2005

Dr. Alcorta,

I just couldn't believe it the other day when I turned the page to see a picture of you!

I am sure you already have a copy of this clipping but just in case, I'm including one.

Thank you so much for everything you do. You are very special.

Blessings,
Missy Mae Walters

Abilene, Texas
May 5, 2008

The card reads: "Having a friend like you . . . *is like having my own personal ray of sunshine!*"
(It is the student's underlining)

Papa Joe,

You have made such an impact on me in the 2 short semesters I have had you as a professor. You provide me with a very bright, positive attitude and outlook on life. Thank you so much for all you are and everything you do! You are such a blessings to everyone you come in contact with! You're my inspiration!

You wife is *so blessed* to have a wonderful, positive, Godly man like you as a husband and leader!

Thank you for being *YOU!*

In His love,
Cheyene
(Jeremiah 29:11)

December 11, 2009

Dr. Alcorta,

I just wanted to say thank you for putting up with me the last few years. Your Christian leadership is something that I hope to model in my own life. Thank you for always having a smile on your face. It was a blessing to come to your class knowing we were going to pray first, and then get on with our work. I will always remember that you were more interested in the student's life than what you had planned for the day. You are a great example for all students and I will never forget "papa Joe." I hope you and your family are blessed in the years to come! I will try to stay in touch as much as I can. Again, thank you for everything!

Sincerely,
Micah Clay

A letter from Dr. John C. Stevens, former president of Abilene Christian University

March 18, 1981

Dear Joe:

Just a note to tell you how much I appreciated the marvelous article Geraldine Satterwhite wrote about you in the Abilene Reporter-News.

And congratulations on the completion of your doctorate.

Joe, I appreciate you as a great citizen, a fine teacher, and a great man. You are strong in the faith.

Please know that your friends at Abilene Christian are thankful for people like you.

Sincerely yours,
John C. Stevens

December 19, 1976

Dear Mr. Alcorta,

I just thought I would drop a line to wish you—Feliz Navidad y un Nuevo año Prospero!

I am teaching bilingual third grade in Levelland, Tex., and have really been learning so much! Your assistance as a Spanish instructor has been invaluable as I have had to use a great deal of Spanish.

This is just a note of thanks, and a congratulations on your new baby.

If you are ever up this way—give us a call!

Best Wishes,
Ann Hubbard

September 24, 2006

Dr. Alcorta,

We look forward to you coming to Howard Payne University to be the Master of Ceremonies for the Alumni Awards Banquet on Friday, October 6 at 7:00 p.m.

As promised, we have a complimentary hotel room for you and your wife at the Comfort Inn in Early. Your confirmation number is below as is the information for the hotel. I'll send you a program draft soon.

Thanks again!

Laura Johnson

My Tribute to Dr. Joe H. Alcorta

I have known Dr. Joe Alcorta since 1960 when he was a freshman in my history class. I have the recollection that at that time he was working at the *Abilene Reporter News* . . . real young . . . interested in everything and always exhibiting a spirit of inquiry into the vast field of learning. He was always in a good humour, always on time to class and always ready to respond to every responsibility placed up him.

I knew him again when he came back to us after obtaining his Master's degree from Howard Payne University. More serious now he was. Ready to begin the journey down the long trail of intellectual achievement that has brought him to the position he has today. Years of responsibility to his family, to his church and to his community never took his eyes off of his own personal voyage of achievement as he pursued his doctoral work. Some years of personal frustration in his studies seemed to only enhance his desire to make the final stage of the journey . . . and now victory is his in this achievement.

I know him now as one of the finest men I have ever known . . . in temperament, in his concern for the needs of others above his own needs . . . in his answering allegiance to the God of heaven and to His glorious Son, our precious Savior and Lord. I count him as a dear precious friend . . . and more than this . . . a brother in the Lord with whom I shall spend all of the glorious years of eternity still set before us as believers. I rejoice that our lives have crossed here and my own life has been blessed by his more than he will ever know.

May our dear Lord overshadow his life and the lives of his dear ones the rest of the way home.

My continuing devotion,
Zane A. Mason, President of the Faculty,
Hardin-Simmons University

My Close Friends

A close friend is difficult to find and to keep. I have hundreds of friends but not too many which are real close. Most of my friends, of course, I have met at work, at church, or at the Rotary club. I would define a close friend as one who you have travelled with, have eaten with, has visited in your home, and feels comfortable with you and your family. And, you have known that person for several years. You, may ask, why so long? Well, people change within a period of time. And with time, the good, the bad and the ugly comes out in a person.

My first close friend who I remember is **Mario Pedroza.** I met Mario in Olton, Texas. It is ironic that his dad and my Dad had actually met back in Monterrey, Nuevo Leon, Mexico in the 1940's. Mario and I rode around in Olton many times. My next best friend was **Mickey Hernandez**. I met Mickey in Olton, Texas, and he and I did a lot of church work together after he became a believer in Jesus Christ. He was a barber. Another close friend from Olton is **Wayne Moore**. Wayne and I worked together at *The Olton Enterprise*. He taught me a lot about the printing business. Wayne, Mickey, and I vacationed in Monterrey, Mexico. We drove in Wayne's new car. Another friend was **Larry Perez** who died at a very young age in a tractor accident. Larry and I drove from Olton to Bronte to see our girlfriends. That night, Becky came back with us so she could marry Larry.

Listed below are a few people and where I have met them who I consider friends. Some are gone or have passed away.

Mision Bautista la Trinidad (Olton, Texas)—Rev. Glen and his wife Oralia Godsey, both deceased now. This is where I met Mickey Hernandez.

The Olton Enterprise (Olton, Texas)—Troy Martin and his wife Korkye; Sue Macon; Gordon Tomkins; Russell Grimes; Wayne Moore;

Gayle McAnally (high school student); Sonny Bryant (high school student); Pat LaFrance, and Eleanor Sudduth.

Ambler Baptist Church (Abilene, Texas)—Eliseo and Audelia Martinez; Elias Cancino; Rev. Paul Vasquez and his wife Beatrice; Alex Vasquez; Rudy and Bettie Morado; Joe and Alice Rios; Richard and Irma Cordero; Robert and Thelma Torres; Gil Torres and all his family

Elmcrest Baptist Church (Abilene, Texas)—Rev. and Mrs. T.C. Melton; John and Barbara Harris; Rev. Dale Suel and his wife Kathy; Felix and Linda Villalovos; Rudy and Judy Fambrough; Earl and Charlie Garrett; Bert and Georgia de la Vega; Jack and Lana Goodridge.

Beltway Park Baptist Church (Abilene, Texas)—Rev. David McQueen, Bob and Jan Clark, Jim and Joy Steadman, John and Verlene Ward, James and Susan Condry, Randy and Marion Voorhees, Max and Connie Deanda; Pete and Doris Linch; Leon and Marion Constable; Jim and Joyce Waddell; Dwight and Della Kinney; Monty and Josie Shy; Chester and Nancy Calhoun; Roddy and Marilyn Haley

Hardin-Simmons University (Abilene, Texas where I have taught for over 40 years)—Jim Alvis, Larry Brunner, Laura Pogue, J. T. Box, Victor Carrillo; Jim Heflin, Alan Stafford, Teresia Taylor, Julian Bridges, Jesse Fletcher, Lanny Hall, Harvey Berlanga; Martha Ferguson; Dorothy Kiser; Zane Mason; Richard Garner; Britt Jones; Brenda Harris; Bob Fink; Larry Fink; Robert Hamner, Dave Gifford, Don Whitmore, Richard Garner, Christi Adams, Britt Jones, Jimmie Keeling, Brad Layton, Frank Loza, Larry McGraw, DeLys Mitchell, Donna Seaton, Dan Stiver, Kathy Williams, Don Williford, Pam Williford, and Larry Wolz.

The Abilene Rotary Club—Peter Agnell, Morris Baker, Jim Bennington, Bruce Bixby, Raymond Blasingame, Tom Boecking, Kim Bosher, J.T. Box, Dave Boyll, Dick Burton, Ed Brokaw, Turner Cariker, Kayla Christianson, Malcolm Coco, George Dawson, Myra Dean, Frank Dlugas, Doug Eichorst, Ray Ferguson, Twyla Foreman, Pete Fox, C.G. Gray, John Harris, Spike Harris, Craig Haterius, Claude Hicks, Fred Lee Hughes, Betty Hukill, Bob Hunter, Erik Johnson, Paul Johnson, Jennifer Kent, Mary Beth Kilgore, Austin King, Charlie Kitchell, Bob Kuykendall, Robert Laird, Bruce Lampert, Paul Lenker, Peggy Manning, James Parrish, Randy Piersall, Marty Pothier, Derral Reed, Buzz Rehm, B.C. Roberson, Richard Rolison, Barbara Rollins, Mike Sadler, Mike Schweikhard, David Stubbeman, Bob Test, Jim Tredennick, Mike Weber, and more.

Printing Shops—Wayne Moore; Joe and Gail Russey; Harry Grant; and Bert de la Vega.

School, business people, boards, committees—Glenn Droomgoole; James Boyd; George Soliz; Lynn Mendenhall.

Of course, **my very best friend is my wife Liandra**. We can talk and discuss just about everything. She is a great listener.

A Sunday Gathering at the Alcortas

It started around the year 2000 that Liandra would cook a family meal on Sunday after church and our children and grandchildren came over to our home at 185 Avenida de Cortez, Potosi, Texas. Charlie Garret, a friend of ours was the real estate agent who sold us the house. The house was built in 1996 by Dave Cannon. Liandra said it was her "dream" house. It had four bedrooms, a large kitchen, a breakfast nook, a dining room, lots of closet space, a wash room, lots of windows; and a three-car garage; plus a huge barn in the back.

I have always enjoyed the fact that Hispanic families are very close. In fact there are many jokes going around about Hispanic families in that grandma and uncles and aunts are always together. If there is a birthday, regardless of the age, everyone is invited. If not, someone's feelings are going to get hurt! Grandma is always invited!!!

Now, as we are creatures of habit let me tell you about the sitting arrangements around the dinner table. I, as the father always sat at the head of the table. Roy Castillo, my son-in-law sat right across me at the other end of the table. To my left sat Joe and then his wife Amber. To my right sat Adriel; next to Adriel was Cecilia. Morgan and Jessica sat to the left of Amber; and Roy and Michael sat to the right and left of Roy. Liandra would normally not sit down; if she did, she sat between Adriel and Cecilia.

As the family grew, we began to bring a second table where the four oldest grandchildren would sit: Roy, Jessica, Michael and Morgan. There was a small round table and chairs for the small children: Ashby, Trey, Drew and Rylie.

Andrew and Kayla and their two little ones lived out of town so they did not come too often. Sarah Alcorta, my sister also began to join us these last two years. Every once in a while Grace Gloria, my niece would also come.

Liandra tried cooking different things; she always wanted to please everyone. (She felt hurt when the children did not like to eat what she had prepared). Here are some typical main dishes she prepared: Carne guisada; Spaghetti with meat; fried chicken, Roast and potatoes; Brisket; Enchiladas, Tacos, Tamales; and T-Bone steaks. For side dishes she would often have pinto beans, Mexican rice, corn, green beans, carrots, macaroni, and a tossed salad.

Every Friday and Saturday Liandra would ask me, "Have you thought of what you want me to make for Sunday?" I would normally give her two or three choices. Many times I would tell her: "Make it easy on yourself."

One thing is for sure: Everybody loved Liandra's homemade flour tortillas. That was one item that everyone agreed on to eat! A fresh hot tortilla with butter is to kill for! Some would literally wait in line to get a fresh tortilla right from the grill ("Comal"). Every once in a while she would not make them, and sure enough, some brave soul would say, "Hey, where are the tortillas?" Once or twice, Jessica and Morgan tried their hand at making tortillas under the direction of Grandma.

Dessert often included fresh strawberries. Jessica loved strawberries. Every once in a while I would go to La Popular (a Mexican restaurant on Pine Street) and buy some Mexican bread. I would buy about a dozen pieces of pan de huevo or conchas. The bread is about 3 inches in diameter, and the top is sugar covered in white, pink, or brown.

Once in a while, Morgan or Michael would bake "Pan Loco." "Pan Loco" is a family tradition that started with my Mother. I once asked my Mother why she called it Pan Loco. She said, "Oh, because I just throw in some flour, sugar, and shortening without measuring; I have no recipe for it." Sometimes someone would bring their birthday cake or the remains of the cake to the lunch. Drinks always consisted of "Cokes," tea, coffee, and water. It was always fun to see Michael drinking sugar with his tea!

To me, the meal was always secondary. I looked for ways to encourage, counsel, and help our family members to grow. One thing, I started doing, I taught the children memory verses in English and in Spanish. Each grandchild gave me a memory verse before I prayed. We started with Michael, Morgan, Jessica and Roy; and then I would work with the smaller children: Ashby, Trey, Drew, and Rylie.

As time passed and the grandchildren grew, each one began to give me a certain one every Sunday. Roy would say, "I can do all thing through Christ who strength me." Jessica would always give me two or three in Spanish: "Todo lo puedo en Cristo que me fortalece," "Dios es Amor," "Jesus lloró," or "Jehová es mi pastor." Michael would say: "Put on the full armor of God so that you can take your stand against the devil's schemes." Morgan continued to surprise me by giving me different ones. The small children together would say: "Children, obey your parents," "Dios es amor," and "Jesus lloró." I would always keep the prayer short because of the children's short attention span; but I always made sure that they would hear that we said thanks to God for our food and our country.

After the meal if anyone had a birthday we would all take turns in saying something good and positive about that person. It was good to hear a brother or a sister say some good things about his/her brother or sister. We also did that on Mother's Day and Father's Day. We asked the children to say some good things about their parents. Some would get a little emotional and sentimental as they talked about their loved ones. I did this because we all need to hear some words of encouragement. That little sentence, "I love you," is still hard to say! Every once in a while we would joke with Cecilia, Roy, Joe and Ambler as they were going to say something good about their spouse. Someone would say, "Okay, get out the Kleenex box!"

After the meal some would read the newspaper and the advertisements. Some would watch a football game, and some would take a much needed siesta. The children loved to play video games, guns, or other games with Uncle Adriel.

Many times I and Adriel would take the children outside to play in the tree house that I had built for them. The tree house had three floors. The basement was ten feet by eight feet and six feet high. They had a fire pole that they could slide from the third floor to the basement. There were three gates to the main floor. There were stairs from the bottom to the second and from second to third.

I also had built swings and two see-saws. For the little ones we had a swing and slide set. Of course the children also like to play in the barn where we had foosball, table tennis, billiard, and a basketball goal.

When I noticed most people were through eating, I would normally begin to clean the table and begin washing the dishes. Liandra did not like for me to wash the dishes. She said I was like a duck throwing water everywhere! Around 4:00 or 5:00 o'clock when everyone was gone, I took a siesta! A long siesta!!!

Our Family Newsletter

In 1974 I shared with Mother that I would like to start a family newsletter. She agreed and we started.

The idea of the "Family Newsletter," (FN) was to keep family members informed of different things that occur in the families. I would be the editor and family members could send Mother or me "their news" that they wanted included in the Family Newsletter.

I have tried to be positive with the FN. We never included any divorces, bankruptcies, or bad news that would embarrass people. Of course, family members eventually find out if so and so divorced, etc. But, they do not find it out in FN.

In the FN we include addresses, e-mails, phone numbers, birthdays, wedding announcements, anniversaries, purchase of new cars, homes, etc. We include accomplishments of school children or promotions or a change of a job. People can write about their vacations or any trips they have taken. Since we have been doing this for several years, we have many newsletters. I have four volumes bound in the following years: **Volume I**—years 1974 to 1985; **Volume II**—years 1986 to 1993; **Volume III**—1994 to 2001; and **Volume IV**—years 2002-2011.

Jeanette Larson, a niece of mine, one of the faithful readers did this acronym for the front cover of **Volume III** of the Family Newsletter.

F—Features family current events.

A—Address book

M—Monthly updates of family

I—Informative

L—Likely to be read before bills

Y—Your family information source

N—Noteworthy news

E—Extra issues for special events

W—Wedding anniversary reminders

S—Special collection of memories

L—Lists upcoming birthdays

E—Entertaining

T—Totally reliable

T—Timely tidbits

E—Edited by Joe H. Alcorta, Sr.

R—Read and treasured by all!

In our annual Alcorta Christmas party (first Saturday after Christmas), I take several bound copies so family members can thumb through them. It always surprises me that I hear different family members, say, "I didn't know that!" or "I had forgotten about that!"

I am including a few articles written in **The Family Newsletter**, from 1974 to 2010 to give readers an idea what type of articles I included in the Newsletter:

June, 1974—Homemaking Award. Ruth Gloria received the Homemaking Award for outstanding achievement in Homemaking for the past year in Olton High School. During the school year she made the "B" honor roll four times and the "A" honor roll one time. For the four year period in OHS, she had an avg. of 83.92. Congratulations Ruth! We are proud of you.

July, 1974—Early Devotional. On July 27th, at 6:00 o'clock in the morning, the Smiths, Martinez, and Alcortas of Abilene had their weekly devotional at Ft. Phantom Lake, followed by a delicious breakfast. It was a great time of fellowship. Gene Smith was in charge of the devotional. Many, many "Coritos" were sung. A baseball game concluded the day's activities. The Lord has really blessed all that have participated, and already many prayers have been answered. Praise the Lord!

August, 1974—Religious concert. Sammy, Anita and Renee Alcorta took "Alpha and Omega" (a singing musical group) from Ambler Baptist Mission to play and sing in Austin and Waco. Josh Martinez plays the guitar for the group.

November, 1974—Officially ordained. Gene Smith and Joe Alcorta were officially ordained as deacons at Ambler Baptist Church on the 10th of November. Gene and Joe answered all the questions very well before the ordination council. The laying of hands during the worship service was very inspirational. It was a unique experience and they will never forget this wonderful occasion. Let us continue to pray for Gene, Joe and their wives so they can continue to serve the Lord.

December, 1974—New members. Sammy and Anita Alcorta are now new church members of Getsemani Asamblea de Dios. Anita is a member of the choir. In the Christmas program she will sing a solo. Sammy will play the part of Santa Claus.

December, 1974—Dear Santa Claus letters from Cynthia Gutierrez; Jeanette Smith; Vickie Garcia; Jimmy Ray Smith; Cecilia Yvette Alcorta; and Angie Gutierrez.

January, 1975—Newly-Weds. On January 14, Ricky Alcorta was married to Frances Coronado of Plains, Texas. Congratulations Ricky and Frances! Welcome to the family, Frances! May the Lord bless their new home. Ricky is working as a butcher in Pay & Save Supermarket in Plains, Texas.

March, 1975—News of the Month. On Monday, March 31, the Lord blessed Pete and Luisa Anzaldua with a baby boy. He weighs 6 lbs. and 7 oz. congratulations Pete and Luisa. May the Lord help you both in guiding and rearing this new baby. The baby and Mother are doing just fine. The father and grandparents are "tickled blue."

April, 1975—To suffer some more! Joe Alcorta wants to express his gratitude for all the people that prayed for him while he took his doctoral exams at Texas Tech. However, the professors want him to suffer some more, so he will have to repeat about half of the exams again around in December. Please continue to pray for Joe (and for Lonnie, so she can put up with Joe!).

September, 1975—New home. Sammy and Anita Alcorta have bought a new house; they sold their house in Abilene, Sammy said what he likes most of this new house is that it has two bathrooms, now he can take his time without being disturbed. Congratulations Sammy, Anita and Rene. They also bought some new furniture for the living room, bedroom, and dining room. Their new address is 5402 Sundown Lane, Garland, Texas 75041.

October, 1975—Cast removed. Cecilia Alcorta has her right hand in full operation again. Her cast was removed on the 29th. She has now learned to write with her left hand also. Talk about one happy little girl!

October, 1975—Death in the family. Longino ("Gino") Villa, Jr. in his early forties passed away on the 7th of October in Chula Vista, California. He was Maria Alcorta's brother. His brother Rafael ("Salvador")

Villa came over to Abilene with Pancho and Rosa Gonzales. He will be working in San Angelo. Let's pray for Gino's widow, Lola, and her two children. Arrangements are in the making to bring them to Abilene or to San Angelo.

July, 1976—Death in the family. We were very sorry to learn that Bartolo Zabaleta, Morena Alcorta's father passed away this month. Let's pray for the Zabaleta family that God will help them through this crisis.

July, 1976—Attends summer camp. Cecilia and Joe Alcorta attended Camp Sunshine for two weeks. It was sponsored by Pioneer Drive Baptist Church. Activities included bible stories, skating, swimming, horseback riding, and other games.

August, 1976—Way up north in Wisconsin. Joe, Lonnie, Cecilia and Joe Jr. Alcorta left Abilene at 7:30 a.m. on August 14th for Ephraim, Wisconsin. They spent the first night in Springfield, Missouri. The next night they spent it with Porfirio ("Pilo") Solis and family in Chicago, Illinois. The next day they arrived in Ephraim, Wis. There they went sight-seeing, swimming, picnicking, boating, and played putt-putt. They said the beaches were out of this world. Michigan Lake was something exciting to see. The weather was near perfect. They rented 2 rooms for $24 a day in this resort area (not bad at all!). A few years ago Lonnie and her family went every year to Ephraim, Wis. for the cherry harvest. Lonnie said it brought her many fond memories . . . .

February, 1977—Jaguar of the month. Cecilia and Joe Alcorta Jr. were selected as "Jaguar of the Month" in their respective grades. The honor means you are courteous to people, you are obedient to your teachers and you finish your work on time. Congratulations C.Y. and "Brother"! We are proud of you.

July, 1978—Run, Run, Run! The jogging and running bug has hit the family. Most any night you will find Martha, Angie, Victor, Cynthia, Joe, Lonnie, Cecilia, Joe Jr., Adriel, Gene, Rachel, Jeanette, and Rozino running at the H-SU track. Some jog, some run, and some walk. Even Ricardo and Maria have circled the track a few times.

November, 1978—Sells 44 tickets. Joe Alcorta Jr. (Brother) won a digital clock radio for selling 44 tickets to the Spaghetti Supper at Johnston Elem. School on Nov. 10. Congratulations Brother!

August, 1979—Softball Champions. Ambler Baptist church Men's Softball team won the YMCA League championship. Their record was 15-1. Gene, Jimmy, and Joe played on the team. Gene played second and Joe pitcher. Jimmy only played part of the time as he was out of town attending classes at Wayland Baptist College. The church won a big beautiful trophy and the players received small trophies.

September 28, 1979—A New Arrival. Joe, Lonnie, Cecilia Yvette, Joe Jr., and Samuel Adriel Alcorta have a new baby in their home. The future tackle of the Dallas Cowboys is Daniel Andres. His weight is 18 pounds (and growing!) at the early age of 5 months. He was born on April 15 in Abilene, Texas in Hendrick Medical Center. The precious, cute, and healthy baby came to live with the Alcorta family on Friday, September 28, 1979 around 10 o'clock in the morning.

April, 1980—"El Carrito" on the Road. "The Nutty Professor" (Joe Alcorta) is again driving his beloved 1941 Chevrolet. Thanks to Ricardo Alcorta and Sammy Alcorta for their help in fixing it. Also, Joe's pastor, the Rev. Paul Vasquez helped a lot. Sammy made the radio work like a new one.

May, 1980—National Honor Retreat. Cecilia Yvette Alcorta had an all-day trip to Seabolt Dude Ranch in Mineral Wells. At the ranch they (The National Honor Society Members) went horseback riding, rode the rapids in the Brazos River and went swimming. This year Cecilia was vice president of the Mann Jr. High Honor Society. Last month, she also participated in a program for the new members.

July, 1980—Three Sisters in College! Can you believe it? Julia Gloria, Martha Gutierrez, and Rachel Smith attended classes at Hardin-Simmons University this past summer . . . and they all passed!!!Let's continue to pray for them as they try to finish their degrees. Girls we all are proud of you because we know how hard it is to have families and then to do the homework.

December, 1980—A Ph.D. in the Family. On December 2, 1980, at 3:00 p.m. at Texas Tech University, Joe H. Alcorta took his final exam in defending his dissertation. The Lord answered many prayers and Joe passed the defense.

January, 1981—Beard growing Contest. Joe H. Alcorta from Abilene has joined the city fathers and is growing a beard to celebrate Abilene's 100 years of existence.

March 11, 1981, EXTRA—Read All About It! Reynaldo (alias Josh) Martinez to lose freedom!!! Berta Luna has won the battle!!!Wonder who will win the war? Josh's Sunday football watching in jeopardy. After August 15, Bernabe and Mague can use the phone again.

April, 1981—First Home Run. Joe Alcorta Jr. has the baseball he hit the first home run of his playing career. The home run came in the first inning with two men on base.

September 2, 1981—Anzaldua's Home Floods as Guadalupe River Overflows. On Tuesday morning of September 1, 1981, Pete and Luisa Anzaldua and family from Cuero, Texas had to evacuate their home.

December, 1981—Joseph Bryan Alcorta is in Heaven. On Saturday, December 26, 1981 at the age of three the Lord took Joseph Bryan to heaven . . . Joseph was very ill for a few days in a Lubbock hospital and then passed away in M.D. Anderson Hospital in Houston after one day's stay. His funeral was in Olton.

May, 1982—Attends Trustee Meeting. Joe H. Alcorta Sr. attended the Valley Baptist Academy trustee meeting in Harlingen. This is his third year to serve as a trustee.

July, 1982—Playing With Angels. As most family members know, little James Richard Smith, 4-year-old, son of Jimmy and Sarah Smith went to live with the Lord and his angels on Wednesday, July 28, 1982. He was buried in Elmwood Memorial Park in Abilene.

August, 1982—It's a Boy! Congratulations to Joe and Debbie Alcorta for their new baby! His name is Jacob Kellen Alcorta. Jacob was born on Tuesday, August 31 at 8:31 a.m. in a Littlefield hospital.

February, 1983—Adriel Alcorta too Sweet! Adriel Alcorta spent 12 days in Hendrick Medical Center in Abilene, Texas for treatment of diabetes. "Diabetes is not an infectious disease. It results from failure of the pancreas to make a sufficient amount of insulin. Without insulin, food cannot be used properly." . . . .

March 14, 1983—Joshua Ryan Smith arrives. There was excitement galore at the Jimmy Smith's home on Saturday, March 12, 1983. It all began with an early phone call from Jimmy's sister-in-law who lives in Big Springs, Texas. She was informing Jimmy and Sarah that the baby they had been expecting for several weeks was soon to be born. Jimmy couldn't get off work from Sears, so Gene, Rachel, and Sarah packed a few pampers and around 10:00 a.m. they head for Big "S" to wait for the arrival of the baby . . . . The trio and baby arrived very tired but happy in Abilene around 10:00 p.m.

May, 1983—Congratulations to the Graduates of 1983: Rachel Smith, H-SU; Pete Anzaldua, Cuero High School; Cecilia Yvette Alcorta, Abilene High School; and Angie Gutierrez, Abilene High.

September, 1983—Captain of the Football Team. Joe Alcorta Jr. has been elected as one of the captains of the 9th grade team at Mann Jr. High. Joe plays free safety on first team on defense, and is the number two QB on offense. Recently he was elected as outstanding player, and he was elected to attend the Abilene High School booster meeting to receive his award and to give a short speech about the Mann Falcons. Congratulations, Joe! Keep working hard.

January, 1984—Meets Roger Staubach in Person. Joe, Lonnie, Cecilia, Joe Jr., and Adriel Alcorta met famous Dallas QB Roger Staubach and got his autograph in Abilene on Tuesday, January 17. Joe Sr. was in the press conference with other reporters before the dinner. Roger was talking to Fellowship of Christian Athletes in Abilene Civic Center.

February, 1984—Time for Cookies Again!!!! Jeanette Smith is again selling those delicious Girl Scout cookies. She is doing very well as a merchant and as a consumer. She has an opportunity to work and earn as much as half of her camp fee for this summer. Let's continue to support her by buying those cookies.

February, 1984—Shape Up Run. On Sat., Feb. 18, Jimmy Smith and Joe Alcorta Sr. ran in the YMCA "Shape UP run." Jimmy ran the 10,000 kilometers (6.2 miles) in 46 minutes, and placed fourth in his age bracket. Joe ran a 51 min. and placed first in his age bracket. Congratulations guys! Keep up the running.

February, 1984—Basketball Champs. Joe Alcorta Sr., Adriel and Andrew saw a very exciting game on Feb. 9th. The Mann Falcons defeated the Madison Bisons for the basketball championship. The game had to go into double overtime. Joe Jr. played very good defense in the last three minutes of the second overtime. The final score was 62-58.

March, 1984—Relay on Biathlon. Joe Alcorta Sr. participated in a relay which consisted of 50 miles on a bike and 26.2 miles on foot. Joe rode the bike 12.5 miles and jogged 6.3 miles. The race started at 7:00 a.m. and it ended around 2:00 p.m. Joe was happy to survive the whole thing.

April, 1984—Annette Anzaldua is Salutatorian of Cuero High School. Pete and Luisa Anzaldua are very proud of their daughter Annette for achieving this great honor. She is the first one in the FN readers to reach this high goal. Three colleges have offered her scholarship.

June, 1984—Martha Marries Charles Willis. The wedding took place on Friday, June 22nd in the home of Jimmy and Sarah Smith in Abilene, Rev. Paul Vasquez performed the double ring ceremony. There was a reception after the wedding. Photographer was Jimmy Smith.

September, 1984—Nice Trip to Italy. Rico and Morena Alcorta had a great time in Italy. The best part was that everything was paid for them! Rico and Morena earned their trip through their work at the store . . . In Italy they visited the ruins of Pompeii, Vatican City, Naples, Florence and the Island of Capri. To get to the island they went by boat.

September, 1984—A War bird at Abilene High School. Joe Alcorta this year is playing safety and quarterback at Abilene High School with about 80 sophomores. Joe has been doing real well playing full time on defense. He is also the punt returner, and plays on the punt and kick-off team. Keep up the good work Joe!

October, 1984—New Scout Leader, Members. Gene Smith has completed some hours in training to become a Scout leader. He is now a leader of troop 5 in which Adriel Alcorta and Dino Smith are members. Good luck to these guys.

January, 1985—Trustee Meeting. Joe Alcorta Sr. attended the trustee meeting of the Baptist Valley Academy in Harlingen, Texas, on January 21 and 22. Joe drove to Dallas and spent the night with Mr. and Mrs. Crespin Chapa; from there he flew to Harlingen and back.

March, 1985—Snow Ski in New Mexico. Victor Gutierrez and Joe Alcorta Jr. had a fun week of snow skiing in Santa Fe, New Mexico. Victor and Joe went with the youth group from Elmcrest Baptist Church. They both had a good time.

September, 1985. Attend Dallas Cowboy Game. Victor Gutiérrez, Joe and Joe Alcorta Jr. had a great time watching in person at Texas Stadium The Dallas Cowboys clobber the old rivals, The Washington Redskins. The score? 44 to 14!! The three Dallas fans went to Dallas with a busload of college students from H-SU. At the beginning of the 4th quarter, the trio found some excellent seats on the 40 yard line to finish watching the game. The guys returned to Abilene at 3:00 a.m.

January, 1986—Esther Sandoval, Sister of Maria Alcorta Passed Away. Esther Sandoval, sister of Maria Alcorta, has gone to live with the Lord. The widow of Alejandro Sandoval passed away in Monterrey, Nuevo Leon on Friday at 1:15 a.m. on the 17th of January, 1986. (Editor's note: How will I remember my aunt Esther? I will always be reminded that she was a very cheerful person. She was a worker and so full of life. She was very attentive and was always willing to give a helping hand. I will recall all the good and fun times we had together while were picking or hoeing cotton in the fields, or while we were working the Whittington Clothing Store in Olton, Texas. She was a lively and vivacious person.)

February, 1986—Play Ball. Congratulations go to Joe Alcorta, Jr. and parents. Joe has made the varsity baseball team at Abilene High School as a right and left fielder. Let's keep Joe in our prayers. Joe and Lonnie took son out to celebrate with a steak dinner.

May, 1986—THE BIG NEWS of the month is Joshua Martinez' graduation from the University of Houston, May 18th. The outstanding event of the decade took place at the Hyatt Regency Hotel in downtown Houston, Texas.

July, 1986—Lots of Fun in Third Family Reunion. The third Ricardo and Maria Alcorta family reunion was a blast! It was held on Saturday, July 5, 1986 at Abilene State Park near Buffalo Gap. It started early in the morning with a continental breakfast, and it continued in different homes till the next day . . . .

August, 1986—Fun Time at Youth Camp. Several cousins had an excellent time at camp in Mt. Lebanon near Dallas on the week of August 11-15. Joe Alcorta Jr was working as sports coordinator and on his staff were Victor Gutierrez, Rene Alcorta and Joe Alcorta Sr. Vic, Rene and Joe Jr. had a fun time staying together in the R.A. Lodge where the rest of the officers stay. Other cousins attending: Cynthia Gutierrez, Vickie Garcia, Delia Cisneros, and Rita Cisneros.

Why I Like Abilene

To Mr. Glen Dromgoole, Editor of *The Abilene Reporter-News* Feb. 17, 1997

I like Abilene because of all the wonderful and friendly people who I have met here in the last thirty-six years. At my work and at my church, I have developed close friendships with many Abilenians, such as my fellowship with the men and women at the Abilene Rotary Club. I enjoy the company and inspiration of my jogging buddies around town.

I love Abilene because I met my wife, Liandra, here. She gave birth to our four children here and seven of our grandchildren were born here. We have planted some roots since we buried our parents here.

I love Abilene because several people in the community have given me and my immediate family an opportunity to work and to develop as individuals.

In Abilene traffic does not create a problem. I travel easily throughout town arriving from point A to point B in less than ten minutes.

Hendrick Medical Hospital has friendly and competent personnel, and our educators care for people.

I enjoy the activities of "Team Abilene" where a mixture of community people come together periodically to help improve the quality of life in our city.

Our teachers, policemen, firefighters, ministers, public workers are the best in the world!

Olivia Velez and her crew at El Fenix of Abilene serve great "Huevos a la Mexicana," which my wife and I have enjoyed for years on our usual Saturday breakfast outing.

I appreciate the editor of *The Abilene-Reporter News* because he has given me and other people in the community an opportunity to express our ideas and feelings about our world by asking us to write guest columns. Thank you Mr. Editor for a great idea!!

Serving as a Translator and Interpreter

In 1971, my very first job outside of the classroom was to do a commercial in Spanish for an optometrist company. I went to the TV studio and my job was to translate from English to Spanish the advertisement. Then I was to record two commercials in a 30 second time limit. If I remember correctly, I was paid $225.00. Not bad, for about 30 minutes of work!

About 1980 on a Saturday afternoon when I was taking my siesta, I received this call from a local business person who had two Mexican customers from Mexico who wanted to buy some farming equipment. The owners did not speak Spanish and the customers did not speak English.

With me serving as an interpreter the two Mexican customers bought around $15,000 that afternoon. I was paid $300.00! Not bad for thirty minutes work! Okay, you can call me again when I am taking my siesta!

Another time I did a sad interpretation in a federal court. I was in front of a federal judge with about 12 illegal Mexicans immigrants. It was sad because most of the men were between 15 and 20 years old. I could tell they were all very scared. The judge was basically trying to find out who was and where was the "coyote." The young immigrants did not know. The judge told me to let them know that they all were going to be sent back to Mexico.

One scary job I did was to go with a lawyer to the French Robinson Penitentiary and interpret for him while he talked to a prisoner about a murder case that had occurred in Lubbock, Texas.

One fun and difficulty job was when I serve as an interpreter for a local Assembly of God church. The guest Hispanic minister was preaching in Spanish and I was right there with him in the pulpit translating to English. I earned my pay that day! Wait a minute . . . did they pay me?

I have served as an interpreter many times for people who go before a judge in trying to be declared physically disable to work so they can apply for Social Security benefits.

I have served in open courts when lawyers are trying different cases. I will interpret for both lawyers and the defendant. I will interpret for the judge as he talks to the person on trial.

I have done many translations in writing. I translated a book, *A Call to Joy* by Dr. Billie Hank. I have translated birth certificates, marriage licenses, dog food labels, cosmetic books, driving handbooks for truck drivers, information to the patient of Hospice of the Big Country and many other kinds of documents.

I Served On The Abilene City Council

I was blessed to have served two terms as an Abilene City Councilman for the City of Abilene. I was elected in April, 1972. The community in which we live gives us a lot, and I felt like everyone should be willing to serve and give back to the community.

I was on the spot. Some minority candidates had previously had been defeated for public office at Abilene and my people were discouraged. I did my best to win so that doors would be open to future Hispanic candidates. I also wanted to prove a premise I had that the mature, educated voter will vote for the qualified candidate regardless of his race or color

I was convinced, even before I ran, that serious voters are not concerned with names like Jones, Smith, Rodriguez or Lopez when balloting, but rather with the candidate's qualifications and I think my election bore me out.

I learned so much when I served those six years. I also had a lot of fun! Few people came to our open meetings. However, one year we were going to have a cat ordinance. Guess what? The place was full! People had been complaining about loose cats in the neighborhood. We were going to suggest that residents call the city when they spotted a stray cat in their yard and the city was to supply them with "a cat trap." People did not accept that!

A second time the place was full when word got out that we were not going to permit recreational vehicles to be parked in front of homes!

A funny and sad incident occurred in the city one day. Joe Loya, a friend of mine, and a long time city employee called me and told me the following: "Joe, I had to shave off my mustache because there is a new rule in the city that no city employee can have a beard or a mustache." Joe was a gentleman and a law abiding citizen. As an Hispanic, Joe probably had his mustache for years. I called J.C. Hunter, our city mayor, and told him about the incident. Well after a few phone calls, the city manager rescinded the ordinance. Joe was very happy about that!

Another funny incident happened that made *The Dallas Morning News*. There was this group in town who wanted to sue the City of Abilene because they were saying that elections were not fair for minorities. They wanted people to be elected from different areas of Abilene. It is known in some cities as Single Member Districts. That day after their lawyer made their presentation to our Abilene City Council our mayor, Fred Lee Hughes answered as he looked at each one of us and said: "Sir, I don't understand how you can say we are discriminating with our elections here in Abilene. On our Council we have a Black (Leo Scott), a Jew, a Mexican-American (that was me), a senior citizen (George Stowe) a woman (Kathy Webster) and an Aggie (Fred Lee Hughes)!" The audience broke into laughter.

Another time the Abilene City Council went on a retreat to the home of one of the councilmen in Brownwood Lake. We went in different cars and as we got off our mayor Fred Lee Hughes was laughing, commenting to me that it was good to be away so that we could do a lot of discussing and business without being worried about the news media. Well, as he and I are talking, I nudge him so he could see who was behind us—Ann Flores, from *The Abilene Reporter News*. Fred Lee, surprised and disturbed at the same time changed facial expressions quick and he said, "Who in the . . . . invited her?" I laughed so much!

My wife and I enjoyed attending the annual Texas Municipal League meetings. It was a good time to meet and spend some quality times with council members and their spouses.

The only time I felt a lot of pressure was when the city voted to sell alcoholic beverages in the city limits. I was strongly against selling liquor in the City and I wrote a letter to *The Abilene Reporter News* expressing my views. After the election passed, some voters were saying that I should not be able to vote in any city ordinance related to liquor since I had been against it.

After my election to the City Council there has been several Hispanics and Blacks who have been elected to serve proudly in the City and in the school board.

Through the years I have enjoyed serving on the following city boards: United Way, Community Action Program, Citizens for a Better Government, Abilene Volunteer Clearinghouse, Abilene High School Role Model Committee, Pregnancy Counseling Service, YMCA, Team Abilene, Serenity House of Abilene, *Abilene-Reporter News* Editorial Board, and The Abilene Teachers Federal Credit Union.

Poem to Honor
Mr. And Mrs. Richard Alcorta, Sr.
On Their Fifty Wedding Anniversary

(In brief, the poem in Spanish by Joe H. Alcorta, Sr.
tells the story of the Alcortas,
how they met, something about their children and grandchildren)

Quincuagésimo Aniversario
(11-21-81)
El viento frio de la noche soplaba
en diciembre del mil novecientos treinta,
cerca de un rancho en el pueblecillo Caps
donde Ricardo Alcorta trabajaba.

Viajando la familia Villa batallaba,
porque el model T marihuana no fumaba.
Refugio pide, y en el rancho se quedaba
donde Ricardo y Maria miraditas se tiraban
y como piensa Maria, el padre Dios obraba.

Un año mas tarde esposos se hicieron;
por varios años en Caps y Novice vivieron.
Seis años en México se divirtieron,
y el cuarenta y seis a Dallas se movieron.
Trece hijos al matrimonio les nacieron,
Maria, Juanito y Enriquito fallecieron.

La mayor es Margarita
que ahora es abuelita;
Julia nace enseguidita
que ya huele a suegrita;
La nena es Raquelita,
que es poco chifladita;
Primer varon es Ricardito
que también es abuelito;
el menor se llama Samuelito
que en la imprenta es jefecito;
Entre medio nace Josecito
que se hizo do(c)torcito;
Se añaden Luisita y Martita
y cada una es mojadita;
La familia es completita
con Irenita y Sarita
que están a dietecita.

Aunque Ricardo ni Maria" cursaron la primaria,
Varios hijos terminaron secundaria
y otros tantos estudiaron universitaria,
y toditos terminaron la primaria.

A medio centenario en el pueblo de Olton,
Julia y Patricio empiezan el desorden,
y el reverendo Godsey los pone en orden.
Mague sigue al casarse con Milton, ministro,
y por años dedican las vidas al servicio.
En ese tiempo se casan Ricardo y Lovelia
los cuales por un tiempo viven en treila.

En la universidad en los sesentas,
José y Lani estudiando se enamoran,
y el cuñado Milton oficia en la boda.
En Olton, apellido cambia Irenita
al casarse con Mariano García
el que cerca gente todo el dia.
Marta se casa con Carlos Gutiérrez

y por veinte años la patria defienden.
Maria Luisa se casa con Pedrito
y ahora toditos viven en Cuerito.

En la iglesia Ambler en los años setentas,
Rachel y Sara se casan con hermanos,
el pícaro Jimmy es maestro y capitán;
Gene, mas calladito sirve al diaconado.
Sammy cambia la marina por las flores
y se casa en Dallas con Anita Flores
quien es bonita, calladita y delgadita.
Romero de Houston le gusta la viudita
y pasa luna de miel con Margarita.

Los nietos alargan el cuento aniversario
y reinan en casa James Richard y Andrés.
Juegan en kinder "Dino" y Adriel.
Jason y Mario principian la primaria;
Jimmy Ray, estudia el año tercero,
aprende y lee en cuarto Jeanette;
Quinto es el grado de Cynthia;
la primaria terminan Victoria y Rene.

En la secundaria de Mann,
Juegan Victoriano y José.
En Abilene, como Aguilas vuelan
Pat Segundo, Esmeralda e Yvette.
Aprenden con los Pavos de Cuero
Pedro segundo y su hermana Annette.
De Olton se gradua Ezequiel;
trabaja y coquetea muy fiel.
A la universidad Graciela va.

Rut, Ricky y Reynaldo leen
los casados de tres erres;
también compañero ya encontraron
Alicia, Laura, Jose, y Benjamin.

De estos nietos casados,
cuatro han engendrado;
por eso Maria y Ricardo
heredan ocho bisnietos chiflados.

Terminemos la historia de medio centenario,
demos gracias al Padre Celestial glorificando,
y felicitemos a este matrimonio cristiano,
porque sufriendo y trabajando por arduos años
hoy celebran su quincuagésimo-aniversario.

Visiting Relatives and Friends

Liandra and I arrived in Wimberley, Texas, on February 20, 2011, to visit Mary, Liandra's sister, and her daughter Marla Burns. Mary works at Wal Mart in San Marcos; and Marla, a Licensed Professional Counselor, works with troubled teenagers on probation. We are staying in this beautiful log house built out here in the country. During the morning around 8:00 a.m., Mary was out behind the house feeding about a dozen deer. The deer were about twenty yards from the back yard. It was a beautiful sight. It had rained the night before so the weather was cold and misty. Four of the deer were eight pointers; the others younger.

One ministry that Liandra and I do is to visit and encourage some of our older friends and relatives. We started visiting Jimmy and Mary back in Ballinger regularly about twenty years ago when Jimmy's health began to fail. Other family members we visit on a regular basis in Mineral Wells are Mike Olivares and his better half, Gwen; and Benita Stokes, in Abilene, who lost her husband Fred about two years ago. We frequently visited Rev. Glen Godsey and his wife Oralia before they passed away.

Liandra and I really enjoy visiting friends and relatives. I always pray with the relatives or friends before leaving their home. The people we visit seem to really appreciate us coming over to visit and to enjoy together a cup of coffee.

Our Saturday Date at El Fenix

A long time ago I learned that married couples should have a regular weekly time together. Well, Liandra and I started going out to breakfast every Saturday morning at El Fenix in Abilene, Texas. We are normally there between 10:00 a.m. and 12:00 a.m. We probably have done this for the last thirty years. From time to time, our children and grandchildren join us for breakfast.

At that time El Fenix was located on 8th street on Treadaway. Olivia Velez, the owner of El Fenix, was the waitress, the cook, and the cashier. Now, February, 2011, Olivia is still in business with a new location in what used to be known as Burro Alley on the corner of South 1st and Willis. She has been in this new location since 1996. At this time, there are many Mexican restaurants, so the competition is stronger.

Olivia and her servers treat us like a king and a queen, and the food is great! And what do Liandra and I order every Saturday? The same thing!!! Normally we order "Huevos a la Mexicana" with coffee. I appreciate Olivia very much because she also carries some of my books which I have written.

This weekly "date" has been good for Liandra and me. Liandra really looks forward to this time. It is always good for us to spend time together. Not only do we enjoy the good breakfast, but we have plenty of time to talk about a lot of things. And, I also take opportunity to pray for our waitress. For years it has become a tradition for me to share with the waitress: "Miss, we are going to say a prayer for our meal, can we include you in our prayer?" Most of the time, the answer is, "Yes, please do!"

Our Cats and Dogs in the Family

Studies have shown that pet animals are good for children. Some authorities say that a pet can help much in the development of a child. I will confess that I don't have a great affection for cats! I am prejudiced! I prefer dogs! I guess because when I was a child we never had a cat! We always had dogs. But, I have never kicked an animal!

In our family we have had several dogs and a few cats. Our first dog was Fluffy, a Collie. He was brown and white. For some reason Fluffy kept running away to my parents' house on 1815 Collins Street (about two miles away). So, we decided for Fluffy to stay with my parents.

Our next dog was Smokey, a Keeshond, charcoal in color. A nurse gave this dog to Liandra. He was real good with Joe and Cecilia. For about fifteen years Smokey protected our home very well at 1518 N. Willis. One sad day was when I had to pick him up from the backyard and take him to the veterinarian so he could be put to sleep. At the vet's office I cried as I said my goodbye's to Smokey.

Our very first cat was Snowball who belonged to Cecilia. Joe was not nice to the cat. One time he swung Snowball around by the tail and threw him in the air to see if he would indeed land on his feet. Sometimes Joe had to climb the backyard tree to get Snowball down as he was chased up the tree by our dog, Smokey. Snowball kept running across the street to our neighbor's house, so eventually, we let the neighbors have the cat.

Our next dog was Rocky, half Lasso and half Pomeranian. Rocky was also a very good dog. He lived with us a long time. Rocky developed a dislocated disk and had to be put to sleep.

Snoopy, was a brown and white Collie dog, which Cecilia found near Hardin-Simmons. Cecilia spent $150.00 with a vet to get him back to good health. However, Snoopy jumped our backyard fence and ran away. We never found him.

My nightmare was Kitty, a Persian cat, given to Joe by sister Cecilia. Andrew had a lot of "fun" with Kitty. He would stuff Kitty in a drawer, and do some other things to the poor cat. Kitty was afraid of Andrew. We had Kitty inside, and she got into a lot of stuff. Her litter box was in the three boys' closet. Needless to say, the room stunk all the time! One day, she scratched a brief case Ambler Baptist Church had given me as a gift. The next thing she did was scratch Joe's dress shoes. Everyone in the family loved her except me!

One day after a week's Bible study, I learned that everything belonged to God. Sounds simple, doesn't it? One summer day as I was jogging, I gave Kitty to God. Sure enough, after a few weeks the family said that if we could find a Christian family that would take her, she could go. Charlene Archer, registrar at Hardin-Simmons at that time, came to our house in her pink Cadillac and took Kitty home! Praise the Lord!

Samson was a black mutt, which belonged to Adriel. Cecilia brought that puppy home from her future in-laws, Mr. and Mrs. Raul Castillo. What I remember about Samson was that he would literally eat anything. He would walk and climb on anything! He kept getting out of the backyard. Our Vet said, "Joe, spray some hot sauce or chili powder all around inside the fence." I did! It didn't work. Samson liked the chili blend!

Samson grew very fat! One day he escaped and was walking down our street, Mrs. Beatrice Vasquez, our pastor's wife, saw Samson and thought he was a pig! Samson developed something in his stomach and he could not digest the food. I took him to the vet to be put to sleep.

When Adriel was little with diabetes, someone gave us Nikko. Nikko, some type of median poodle, was a classy dog and very obedient. This dog quickly bonds with children. Well, Nikko got attached to Adriel, and Nikko would sleep with him. In the morning when I would go and try to wake up Adriel, Nikko would growl at me. He would not let me get close to Adriel. Nikko lived with us for a long time, and like anything else, he got old! It got to where Nikko could not see or hear very well. He was having a rough time.

Well, it happened! One day when I was getting ready to go to HSU and, somehow, Nikko got out from the front door and went and lay behind a tire of my van. It was awful! I backed out and ran over Nikko! Oh, my! I was nervous, scared, and I felt terrible! The first thing that came to my mind, was, "How am I going to tell Adriel?" Well, at noon, I came back to the house and buried Nikko in the backyard. Adriel was very understanding. He told me, "Dad, I know it was an accident, what did you do with him?"

Adriel placed a wooden marker in a bone shape with the words, "Nikko, may you rest in peace."

Later on, Adriel bought a Dalmatian from my friend Paul Lenker. It was a big dog. Then somehow or other Andrew came across another huge dog, a Pit Bull. We had two huge dogs in the back yard, and I saw them as a danger to our small grandchildren. I finally convinced Adriel and Andrew to give up their dogs. I found someone that wanted them.

Our next dog was Missy. The black poodle was given to Joe by Amber's parents, Mr. and Mrs. Billy Burton. She spent most of her life with us at 1518 N. Willis. She also was an inside dog. Missy was also very obedient. She ended up being very attached to Adriel. She came with us to our new home at 185 Avenida de Cortez. Missy was also very obedient.

Missy grew old with us. She could not see, hear, or control her bladder. Liandra would get very upset when Missy would mess up in the bathroom where she stayed. Adriel and I had decided that perhaps it was time for Missy to be put to rest, but he often had second thoughts. Finally, one day, Adriel told me that it was time, and I took her to our friend, Dr. Lynn Lawhon, a veterinarian

Last year, 2010, another dog, Winston, was given to us by a nurse who worked at Hendricks. It was a well-groomed, high class dog, very white in color. I should have gotten a hint when Adriel and I went to pick him up. A teenage girl was holding him, and I asked her, "Are you willing to give him up?" She said, "Yes." The mother said that they did not have time for the dog and that the teenage daughter was not feeding him, etc. The nurse also said Winston was afraid of men, and that she thought the dog had probably been abused before coming to their home.

Well, it was sad but Winston did not work out. He growled at Ashby and attacked Adriel twice, and he could not control his bladder. Again, I made a trip to Dr. Lawhon's office who had advised us to put the dog to sleep.

And the animal stories continue with Andrew, our youngest son, who became the owner of a registered black female Labrador while living in Huntsville. Andrew resigned his job and came through Abilene before moving to Dallas. He brought the Labrador, Shadow, to our place while they found an apartment in Dallas.

About six weeks ago in January 2011, Shadow surprised us and gave birth to eight puppies. Two did not survive. We don't know who the father is, but he is probable, some happy dog back in Huntsville. While they were about four weeks old, we had snow and ice at our place. At night, it got around eight degrees. Adriel brought the puppies in for protection, and he put Shadow in the barn. They cried nearly all night long!

We gave one puppy to a friend of Mrs. Roy Castillo. That left five! On a Sunday afternoon, February 13, we loaded them up in a cage in Joe's pickup and drove to town and parked near the Olive Garden. Adriel, Ashby, Michael, Trey, and myself were there about two hours. Michael had made the sign: "Free Puppies." Ashby and Trey were holding up the sign. Several people stopped by to see, admire, and pet the puppies. Some people could not believe the puppies were free. Soon they were all gone! Oh, yes, Adriel and Ashby kept one white puppy.

Adriel had Shadow tied up but felt sorry for the dog, and he let her loose. She did not run away, but it seems likes she was getting into people's yards and creating some problems. We received a few nasty calls from our neighbors. So, now Shadow is tied up and inside a fenced area behind our home.

Back to the cats! Mindy Wheeler, a former student of mine through e-mail at HSU offered two cute kittens to whoever wanted them. Since we had moved out to the country, 185 Avenida de Cortez in Potosi, someone had told me that we needed cats to protect us against snakes!!

Joe and Amber also brought us two kittens, which came from their friends' home. Well, the cats multiplied, and at one time, we had more than twenty! Some were good; some were bad. We gave some away to Mike Olivares, Liandra's brother. I took one to Stamford to fight mice in a grain barn.

There were several problems with the cats. The odor, the litter boxes, and the cats get into everything! Our daughter, Cecilia, and some of our grandchildren are allergic to cats. Recently, Jerry Bingham, our P.A. told Adriel to get rid of the cats as they were causing him allergy problems. We lost some cats to the coyotes, some ran away, and some we gave away. We finally were down to five grown cats, which we kept in the garage to protect them from the cold and the coyotes.

Recently, February 2011, I ran across Paul Washburn at Dale's Barbershop. Paul is the CEO of Rescue the Animals. I told Paul about our cats; he gave me the go ahead to bring them to his place and that they would find foster homes for the cats. So, a few days ago, we loaded them up in a cage in Joe's pickup and delivered the cats safely to Rescue the Animals. Now we have left Shadow and three other dogs.

Even though the above cats and dogs caused me misery and lot of problems, I would probably do it over again. My wife likes cats and dogs. My children and grandchildren also like them. I know these animals have brought a lot of happiness to our family. It has also taught our children and grandchildren responsibility.

One of my Typical Classes at Hardin-Simmons

Our bread and butter classes in The Foreign Language Department are Elementary and Intermediate Spanish. Every semester I teach at least one Elementary and one Intermediate class. Through the years I would also teach Advanced Spanish Grammar, Spanish Conversation, and Hispanic literature classes.

This is what I normally do: I have the students fill out a 3 X 5 index card and ask them to give me their name, phone number, e-mail address, classification, major and minor, and their hobbies. On the back of the card I ask the student to list at least 5 long time goals. I tell them: "People, who write down their goals, are the people who will probably complete their goals."

The first day of class I will tell them: "To succeed in this class and in life, I think the following things will help you: 1) in everything you do, put God first in your life; 2) be a positive person; 3) be a disciplined person; and 4) learn to have fun in life."

I lead in a prayer the first day of class. We always pray on Mondays and Tuesdays, and I ask the students before prayer for three things: 1) does anyone have a prayer request; 2) does anyone have a blessing they would like to share with the class; and 3) does anyone have a Scripture they would like to share with the class.

I will always have the index cards with me and they help me to call on students. All through the class period I keep shuffling the cards; and I call on students at random. They never know when I am going to call on them.

My philosophy is that students learn by doing. So, I strongly encourage students to repeat practical sentences that they would use outside of the classroom. I try very hard to understand and comprehend my students; I try very hard not to embarrass them.

From time to time I tell my students "Teaching Spanish to you is my secondary goal. My main goal is to somehow, in some way to lead you, and teach you how to become a solid responsible and successful, and productive citizen."

We try to have fun in the class. When we study foods, I will always ask, what is the food that you do not like at all; and what is the food that you could eat every day? With clothing I do the same; and I will ask them to comment on "Clothes make the man/woman."

When we study about family members, I ask them to describe their Mom, Dad, Grandpa, and themselves. I ask about parents. Who is the spender and who is the one who saves? Who is the one who has patience and who is the impatient one? Are you like your Mom or your Dad?

From time to time I encourage students to attend different university functions. I tell them, "Don't graduate without ever having attended a football game, or a basketball game, or a baseball game, or a soccer game, or a play, or a concert."

I really enjoy teaching literature classes because you can teach so much about life as you talk about the characters in a poem, a short store or in a novel. We have great discussions in the classroom.

On Fridays, I ask the students to bring a 3 X 5 index card with a quote, a proverb, or a Scripture. I suggest: ask your Mom, your Dad, or your Grandpa what their philosophy of life is and write it on the card. We spend the last five minutes of the class reading these cards. The comments on the cards create good discussions.

Generally speaking, I have had great students in my classes. The majority of my students have always tried to do their best. The few students who have failed my classes have failed because of poor attendance, or because they just quit coming to class. I tell them, "You or your parents are paying too much money to fail this class!"

Teaching Sunday School

As an adult, I have always taught a Sunday school class in every church I have been a member. I strongly believe a Sunday school class is where a person learns more about the Bible and God. It is also through Sunday school that a person can grow and mature as a believer. In a Sunday class a person has the opportunity to ask questions and to share one's testimony. I would estimate that less than 50% of church members attend a Sunday school class on a regular basis.

Here is what I normally try to do in our Sunday school class. I will greet everyone by hand with a smile, and if available, enjoy coffee with class members. If someone brings doughnuts, I never turn them down! I like for class members to sit in a semi—circle so they can see each other. I encourage everyone to know everyone by name. From time to time I have class members introduce each other and to say something about their families and work.

I will ask class members if they have a birthday, an anniversary, or a prayer request. I then ask for two or three volunteers to pray out loud. Our Sunday school lessons normally come from a Lifeway quarterly; on the board I will write the tile of the lesson and where the Scriptures are found.

I will ask volunteers to read from the Bible, and then I will explain verse by verse. I encourage class members to participate and to ask questions in our discussions. I tell my students, "I believe the Bible from cover to cover." I also add jokingly, "If the Bible should say that Jonah ate the whale (fish) I would believe it too."

I know that through the years I have lost some class members because they disagree with some of my teachings. Through my teaching, class members soon learn that I do not drink, smoke, gamble, or play the lottery. I teach what the Bible says about abortion and divorce, but I also teach that God forgives any sin. I believe what the Bible says in I John 1: 9: "If we confess our sins, he is faithful and just and will forgive us ours sins and purify us from all unrighteousness." I try to have fun in the class. I share a lot of personal stories to encourage and to help class members become more and more like Jesus.

As of March 2011, here are my current Sunday school class members at Beltway Park Baptist Church: Jim and Joyce Waddell; Jim and Joy Steadman; Dolly Carpenter; Leon and Marion Constable; Theda Goodrich; Patsy Kelsey; Phil and Debbie Miller; Max and Connie Deanda; Pete and Doris Linch; Jackie Barton; Roddy Haley; Jose Soto; David Harmon and my wife Liandra.

As well as teaching a Sunday school class, I also enjoy teaching a men's class. For the last ten years I have taught a men's class on Wednesday nights. Besides reading Scripture and praying, we have studied many books related to men's needs. Normally we start class with coffee and dessert. We read a Scripture and pray. We then discuss the topic of the night from whatever book we are studying. Listed are my current class members: Max Deanda, Jim Steadman, John Ward, Bob Clark, and Don Healow.

As most teachers know, a teacher learns much when he teaches. I have learned so much about the Bible and God. These men and women often challenge me to study more. It has been a tremendous blessing being associated with all these men and women.

My Favorite Scriptures

One of my favorite past times is reading. After graduating from Hardin-Simmons, I began to read on a daily basis. My Mother started sharing pamphlets from Dr. Norman Vincent Peale which she received in the mail. Besides reading his pamphlets and other materials I read his book, *The Power of Positive Thinking*. This book helped me a lot. But no other book has influenced my life like the Bible, God's Holy Word.

I grew up in a Christian home, but I don't think I was real serious about reading God's Word. I read the Sunday school lessons like a normal church goer. My serious Bible reading and studying began when I was around 40. It was Brad Waggoner, one of the pastors at Elmcrest Baptist Church who encouraged and challenged me to memorize Scripture. Chuck Swindoll's book, *Living Beyond the Life of Mediocrity* also encouraged me to memorize Scripture.

Jesus' Sermon on the Mount, found in Matthew chapters 5, 6, and 7, is outstanding. Jesus' last words to His disciples found in John 14-17 are also powerful and tremendous instructions for Christian living. Of course, Romans chapter 12 has really challenged my life. If you cannot find time to read the whole Bible, make a big effort to read Matthew 5, 6, and 7, John 14-17, and Romans 12. These Scriptures will challenge you in a great way. Of course, the book of Psalms is excellent for worship or daily prayers. The book of Proverbs has many ideas for daily Christian living. It covers many subjects: money, women, work, and marriage.

For years I have read Proverbs. Look at the calendar. Whatever date it is, read that Proverb for the day. Do that for the month, and repeat month after month. If you do not have time to read the whole chapter, then read just one verse.

Here are just a few Scriptures that I have put to memory, and they mean much to my life:

"This book of the law shall not depart from your mouth, but you shall meditate on it day and night, so that you may be careful to do according to all that is written in it; for then you will make your way prosperous, and then you will have success."

—Joshua 1: 8.

The idea here is to think about God's Word continually and to do what it says—in order to obtain success.

❧

"Have I not commanded you? Be strong and courageous! Do not tremble or be dismayed, for the Lord your God is with you wherever you go."

—Joshua; 1: 9

Remember, do not be afraid, God is always with you.

❧

"and My people who are called by My name humble themselves and pray, and seek My face and turn from their wicked ways, and then I will hear from heaven, will forgive their sin, and will heal their land."

—II Chronicles 7: 14

If we pray daily and keep away from evil God will hear our prayers.

❧

"Yet those who wait for the Lord will gain new strength; they will mount up with wings like eagles, they will run and not get tired, they will walk and not become weary."

—Isaiah 40: 31

Waiting on God is hard, but that is what we need to do to get stronger.

☙❧

"**Do not fear, for I am with you; do not anxiously look about you, for I am your God. I will strengthen you, surely I will help you, and surely I will uphold you with my righteous right hand.**"

—Isaiah 41: 10

God is always with us, and He will help us. Do not give up.

☙❧

"**For My thoughts are not your thoughts, Neither are your ways My ways,**" declares the Lord.
"**For as the heavens are higher than the earth, so are My ways higher than you ways, and My thoughts than your thoughts.**"

—Isaiah 55: 8, 9.

Sometimes we cannot understand God because we cannot think or act as He does.

☙❧

"**For I know the plans that I have for you, declares the Lord, plans for welfare and not for calamity to give you a future and a hope.**
Then you will call upon Me and come and pray to Me, and I will listen to you.
And you will seek Me and find Me, when you search for Me with all your heart."

—Jeremiah 29: 11-13.

The Lord always wants the best for us, but He wants it done His way.

ᧁᕝᧁ

"Bring the whole tithe into the storehouse, so that there may be food in My house, and test Me now in this," says the Lord of hosts, "if I will not open for you the windows of heaven, and pour out for you a blessing until it overflows."

—Malachi 3: 10

This commandment is with a promise. Give ten percent to the church, and the Lord will bless you.

ᧁᕝᧁ

"But seek first His kingdom and His righteousness; and all these things shall be added to you."

—Matthew 6: 33.

God always wants to be first in our lives. When that happens, the rest of the stuff will take care of itself.

ᧁᕝᧁ

"For God so loved the world, that He gave His only begotten Son, that whoever believes in Him should not perish, but have eternal like."

—John 3: 16.

This is the heart of the Bible. God loves us so much that He gave His Son for us.

ᧁᕝᧁ

"Rejoice in the Lord always; again I will say, rejoice!"

—Philippians 4: 8.

Paul was in prison when he wrote these words. We are to be happy.

෧༚෨

"Be anxious for nothing, but in everything by prayer and supplication with thanksgiving let your requests be made known to God. And the peace of God which surpasses all comprehension shall guard your hearts and your minds in Christ Jesus."

—Philippians 4: 5, 6

Don't worry about anything! Tell God about it and forget it!

෧༚෨

Finally, brethren, whatever is true, whatever is honorable, whatever is right, whatever is pure, whatever is lovely, whatever is of good repute, if there is any excellence and if anything worthy of praise, let your mind dwell on these things."

—Philippians 4: 8.

Think only about the good things in life.

෧༚෨

"Do not love the world, or the things in the world. If anyone loves the world, the love of the Father is not in him. For all that is in the world, the lust of the flesh and the lust of the eyes and the boastful pride of like, is not from the Father, but is from the world."

—I John 2: 15, 16.

Do not love things and evil things.

❦

"and He shall wipe away every tear from their eyes; and there shall no longer be any death; there shall no longer be any mourning, or crying, or pain; the first things have passed away."

—Revelation 21: 4.

I like this Scripture a lot!!! When we are in heaven, there will be no more death, mourning, crying, or pain!

Conclusion

I hope and pray that the reading of the book will encourage people in their everyday living. Few things in life come easy. Every person has obstacles to overcome. With hard work, determination, and persistence, many things can be accomplished.

Elementary, high school, and college classes were hard for me. I did not have a high I.Q. or educated parents who could help me with my homework. We did not have a set of encyclopedias, and it was not until later in life that we had a dictionary in our home. My parents, however, did encourage me in school. They always wanted me to do my very best, and I did not want to disappoint them.

From an early age, I was taught to always put God first in my life, to work, and to respect people. My parents also took me to church. In church I learned more about God, worship, prayer, and relationships.

We live in a great country. We need to work hard to keep it that way. There are millions of people that would love to see us fail. Teach your children and grandchildren how to respect and defend our country. This country is truly the land of opportunities. Let us take advantage and fulfill our greatest dreams.

I am thankful first to God for what He has done for me and our family. I am also thankful to my parents, my wife, my children, my brothers and sisters, my teachers, and my friends for helping me to accomplish many of my dreams.

Dear reader, you too can fulfill your dreams. I challenge you to dream big. With God and support from family and friends you can accomplish your biggest dreams. Go for it! As Zig Ziggler's book title reads, "*See You at the Top*."

Other Books by Dr. Joe H. Alcorta

1. Historia de la Iglesia Ambler, 1982
   (A History of Ambler Baptist Church)
2. Historia de un Famoso Equipo: Los Dallas Cowboys, 1989
   (A History of a Famous Team: The Dallas Cowboys)
3. Speak Spanish in 60 Days, 1990 (includes CD)
4. The (Almost) true Story of a Church committee, 1992
5. Essential Spanish for Bankers, 1999
6. Essential Spanish for Doctors and Nurses, 1999
7. Essential Spanish for Policemen, Lawyers, and Judges, 2000
8. Essential Spanish for Teachers and other School Personnel, 2001
9. Essential Spanish for Restaurant Personnel, 2006
10. Essential Spanish to Share Your Faith, 2008
11. A Collection of Hispanic Proverbs and Sayings, 2005
12. Words of Wisdom from a Cool College Professor, 2010.

Our family; back (l-r) Joe, Andrew; front (l-r) Cecilia, Liandra, Joe, Adriel

Joe H. Alcorta at Abilene High School, 1967, mimeograph machine;
making copies for class

Joe H. Alcorta and a former student, Travis Seeking, October, 2010,
after completing a marathon.
Travis first in full marathon; Joe first in ½ marathon.

That's me cooking those famous pancakes for our
Annual Alcorta Christmas Party in 2006

Me and my Buick in 1956

Me and my Mother, Maria, at Mision Bautista la Trinidad
with my first place ribbon which I won in Number Sense

My daughter and three grandchildren ran the McMurry 5K on November 2010. (l-r) Roy Castillo, Cecilia Castillo, me, Michael Castillo, and Morgan Alcorta.

That's me in the middle (No. 2908) running the Dallas White Rock Lake Marathon on December 7, 1997. My best time in the marathon was 3 hours and 45 minute. Not bad for a senior citizen!

That's me and bride Liandra with our parents in First Christian Church,
Breckenridge, Texas, on August 19, 1962.
On the left are Mr. and Mrs. Miguel Olivares, and on the right are
Mr. and Mrs. Richard Alcorta.

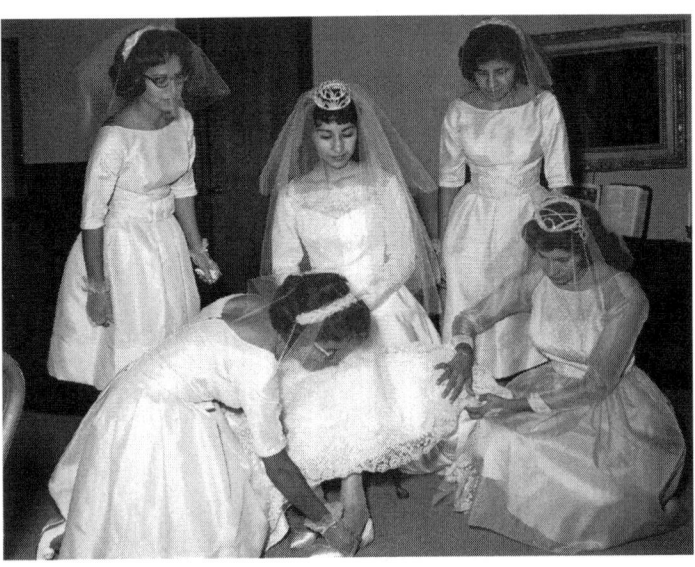

That's my bride Liandra getting dressed. Standing (l-r) are Martha Alcorta and
Priscilla Rojas; kneeling are Luisa Alcorta and Benita Olivares.

My boss Victoriano ("Tano") Gutierrez on top of a trailer
in the Olton cotton fields in 1951.

Two tough "hombres!" (L-r) Irene and husband Mario Garcia;
Luisa and husband Pete Anzaldua.

Three brothers. (L-r) Richard, me, and Sammy Alcorta.
Picture taken at Richard's home (Plains, Texas), on July 4, 1999.

Dr. Ken Jacobs and me on April 16, 1998. Ken taught history at
Hardin-Simmons. Here we are "working" at campus with Western Heritage
Days where around 2,000 local elementary children visit the campus.

I grew up with seven sisters! (L-r) Margarita Greaves, Julia Gloria, Luisa Anzaldua, Martha Gutierrez, Sarah Smith, Irene Garcia, and Rachel Smith.

Children and grandchildren of Joe and Liandra Alcorta.

- Front on the floor (L-r): Rylie Alcorta, Andrew Alcorta, Trey Castillo, Ashby Alcorta, and Adriel Alcorta.
- Seating (L-r): Michael Castillo, Joe Alcorta, Liandra Alcorta and Roy Castillo.
- Back row (L-r): Andrew Alcorta, Kayla Alcorta, Roy Castillo, Cecilia Castillo, Joe Alcorta, Morgan Alcorta, Amber Alcorta, and Jessica Alcorta. (photo taken, June, 2010, Caleb Alcorta not in picture)

Grandchildren of Joe and Liandra Alcorta. (Front-back): Rylie Alcorta, Roy Castillo, Jessica Alcorta, Michael Castillo, Morgan Alcorta, Ashby Alcorta, Trey Castillo, and Andrew Alcorta. (Not in the picture is Caleb Alcorta, 13 years old) Photo taken, June, 2010.

Joe and Liandra Alcorta entering their home (photo taken, June, 2010)

Me and my two brothers, picture taken in 1968? (L-r) Joe H. Alcorta, Richard Alcorta, and Sammy Alcorta. Sammy made the family proud by serving in the U.S. Marines; "Rico" worked many years as a grocery store manager.

That's me in the classroom teaching Spanish at Abilene High School in 1966

Visiting home in Olton with my parents,
in my ROTC uniform, Mr. and Mrs. Richard Alcorta
Picture taken in April 1961.

That's me in 1947 in a cotton field in Olton, Texas.
In a good day I could pull 1000 pounds!

That's me relaxing on my 55 Chevy in front of Ferguson Hall at
Hardin-Simmons in 1960.

That's me in front of my 55Chevy in Olton, Texas, 1959.

They say "A picture is worth a thousand words." This is my Grandson Ashby
Alcorta at 14 months old, behind in our home at 185 Avenida de Cortez calling
our dog, Missy. In the background is my pride and joy where I Spend many
hours working on woodwork.

I beat them all in 1991 in this 5K at Hardin-Simmons. (L-r) Victor Gutierrez, a friend of Victor, Andrew Alcorta, Me, Joe Alcorta Jr., Cecilia Castillo, Adriel Alcorta, and Rozino Smith

My brother and sisters in Plains, Texas cemetery. This picture was taken on May 9, 2008, the day of the burial of our sister-in-law, Morena Alcorta. From (L-r) are Irene Garcia, Luisa Anzaldua, Margarita Greaves, Martha Alcorta, Joe H. Alcorta, Sarah Alcorta, and Sammy Alcorta.

This is Mr. Harry Ford and me in Littlefield, Texas, on January, 2005. Family and friends were celebrating Mr. Ford's 95 years of life. Mr. Ford was my Algebra, Plane Geometry, and Physics teacher in Olton High School, Olton, Texas.

Edwards Brothers Malloy
Ann Arbor MI. USA
May 31, 2016